THE KILLER
MOUNTAINS

BOOKS BY
Curt Gentry

THE DOLPHIN GUIDE TO SAN FRANCISCO
AND THE BAY AREA:
Present and Past

THE MADAMS OF SAN FRANCISCO

JOHN M. BROWNING: AMERICAN GUNMAKER
(with J. Browning)

THE VULNERABLE AMERICANS

FRAME-UP

Curt Gentry

THE KILLER MOUNTAINS

A Search for the Legendary Lost Dutchman Mine

André Deutsch

For Coronado's Children

First published 1971 by
André Deutsch Limited
105 Great Russell Street
London WC1
Copyright © 1968 by The New American Library, Inc.
All rights reserved
Printed in Great Britain by
Lowe & Brydone (Printers) Ltd
London
ISBN 0 233 96169 0

A Warning:

There is something in a treasure that fastens upon a man's mind. He will pray and blaspheme and still persevere, and will curse the day he heard of it, and will let his last hour come upon him unawares, still believing that he missed it only a foot. He will see it every time he closes his eyes. He will never forget it until he is dead . . . and even then he will pass it along to his survivors, that they may follow in his footsteps. There is no way of getting away from a treasure . . . once it fastens itself upon your mind.

Joseph Conrad,
NOSTROMO

Contents

Prologue	1
CHAPTER 1 Was There a Dutchman?	5
CHAPTER 2 In Search of Cañón Fresco	18
CHAPTER 3 Seven Glittering Cities of Gold	41
CHAPTER 4 Murders, Disappearances, and "Accidental" Deaths	74
CHAPTER 5 "Veni, Vidi, Vici"—The Death of Adolph Ruth	94
CHAPTER 6 The Secret of the Maps	108
CHAPTER 7 An Insurance Policy	119
CHAPTER 8 The Tunnel and the Pit	129
CHAPTER 9 What To Do with a Gold Mine?	151
CHAPTER 10 The Vanishing Pit	179
Epilogue	195
Index	206

Illustrations
FOLLOWING PAGE 118

The first Peralta-Ruth map

Needle Canyon

Map showing Peralta's route from Mexico

Map showing Lost Dutchman Mine

Andy Vloedman breaking Satan

Andy Vloedman, Carl Lee, Satan, Pauline, and Baker Looney

Bluff Springs Mountain

Needle Canyon from the tunnel area

Glenn Magill

The pit above the tunnel

Bill Young in the Arizpe cemetery

Copperhead found outside Magill's motel room

Glenn Magill's own map

Prologue

A FEW MINUTES after 8 A.M. on Friday, April 29th, 1966, the teletype of United Press International sounded its warning bell, then began a rhythmic clacking. In city rooms across the United States copyboys tore off the long yellow sheets.

Some automatically spiked them on wire spindles. Others quickly scanned the lines.

Among those who read the words, reactions varied.

A few grinned and thought, "Now where have I heard that before?"

Others felt vaguely disappointed, for far back in their memories lurked youthful hopes of someday being the ones to make the discovery.

And still others, almost unconsciously, for all their pretended cynicism, felt a thrill of excitement, imagining the real story behind the lines.

1

FABLED GOLD MINE (CAPS)
6 SAY THEY FOUND (CAPS)
'LOST DUTCHMAN' (CAPS)
OKLAHOMA CITY (UPI)
A PRIVATE INVESTIGATOR SAID YESTERDAY THAT HE AND FIVE ASSOCIATES HAD DEFINITELY LOCATED THE LEGENDARY LOST DUTCHMAN MINE (CAP L,D) IN ARIZONA'S SUPERSTITION MOUNTAINS (CAPS).

"WE DON'T THINK WE HAVE THE RIGHT MINE," SAID GLENN MAGILL, "WE KNOW WE DO."

MAGILL SAID THE GROUP HAD USED MAPS OBTAINED FROM A MAN WHOSE FATHER WAS SLAIN IN THE SUPERSTITION MOUNTAINS 35 YEARS AGO. HE SAID THEY HAD REMOVED NUGGETS FROM THE MINE AND FOUND THEM TO BE "ALMOST PURE GOLD."

RICHES

"I BELIEVE THE MINE IS EVEN RICHER THAN ANYONE CAN IMAGINE," MAGILL SAID. "THE DUTCHMAN SAID IT HAD THE WEALTH OF MANY MINES. I DON'T BELIEVE HE FULLY UNDERSTOOD HOW WEALTHY IT REALLY WAS."

HE SAID THE MAPS AND NUGGETS WERE KEPT IN A SAFE DEPOSIT BOX AND WERE NEVER CARRIED BY THE SEARCHERS.

MAGILL SAID HE AND HIS ASSOCIATES WERE CHECKING THE LEGAL STATUS OF THEIR FIND AND WOULD NOT REVEAL ITS LOCATION EXCEPT THAT IT WAS IN A GOVERNMENT WILDERNESS AREA.

CLUES

"IT'S JUST EXACTLY WHERE THE DUTCHMAN TOLD EVERYBODY IT WAS," HE SAID. "IT'S RIGHT ON THE SPOT. HE LEFT MANY CLUES TO THE LOCATION AND EVERY ONE OF THEM CHECKED OUT."

HE SAID THE GROUP HAD LOCATED CAMPS OF THE DUTCHMAN, A GERMAN IMMIGRANT NAMED JACOB WALTZ WHO DIED IN PHOENIX IN 1891.

MAGILL SAID HE HAD OWNED ONE MAP FOR SEVERAL YEARS

AND OBTAINED THE OTHER THREE ABOUT FOUR MONTHS AGO FROM DR. ERWIN RUTH, OF WASHINGTON, D.C., SON OF ADOLPH RUTH, WHO WAS MYSTERIOUSLY SLAIN IN 1931 WHILE SEARCHING FOR THE LOST MINE.

What happened before, and after, this story appeared is the subject of this book.

CHAPTER 1

Was There a Dutchman?

GLENN MAGILL did not set out to find the Lost Dutchman Mine. Rather, when the 37-year-old Oklahoma City private investigator began his search in 1964, he hoped to prove that neither the mine nor its legendary founder had ever existed.

Born in Indianola, Oklahoma, in 1927, the son of a Barnum and Bailey clown who had retired from circusing to become a Deputy U.S. Marshal, Glenn Magill had known more than the usual share of boyhood adventures. But, like any other youth raised amid the legends and lore of the American Southwest, one thing above all others had especially caught and held his fancy—the lost bonanza and buried treasure tales.

There was Pegleg Smith's lost lode in California, the Lost Gunsight in Nevada, Billy the Kid's loot and the Lost Adams Diggings in New Mexico. Even closer to home, in Oklahoma itself, were the hidden caches of the James gang, the Daltons, and a half-dozen other outlaw bands. Of all the legends, however, the best known—the giant of them all—was that of the pit and tunnel in the mysterious Superstition Mountains in Arizona: the legendary Lost Dutchman Mine.

Like his fellows, the Oklahoma youth had dreamed that one day he—Glenn D. Magill—would find it.

But with the passage of time, one usually outgrows such dreams, or replaces them with others more practical. During World War II, Magill had run away from home to join the Navy. (As a missing-person case, it was remarkably short-lived; his age was discovered and he was back home within three months.) And after he finished high school, other dreams and responsibilities had moved in. Although he hadn't given the Lost Dutchman Mine much thought since boyhood, he was aware, from periodic newspaper stories, that many grown men had spent their lives searching for it. Literally. Rarely had a year passed without an account of one or more deaths within the confines of the "killer mountains." The curse of the Apache Thundergods, or so said the legend.

J. Frank Dobie called them "Coronado's Children," these modern-day seekers after myths. To the private detective, trained to deal with proven facts, the appellation was eminently suitable. He thought of these men as perennial adolescents.

His connection with the search began routinely enough, with an assignment from a Denver attorney to locate the heirs to a uranium claim. Finding missing persons had been a specialty of Glenn Magill & Associates since its inception in the 1950s. The search, which lasted two months and took Magill and his operatives over a half-dozen states, ended in Dallas with the successful identification of the last heir. To celebrate, the attorney invited Magill and his wife, Melba, to dinner.

"You know, Glenn," he remarked, opening the second bottle of champagne, "with your investigative techniques, and my knowledge of its history, I'll bet we could find the Lost Dutchman Mine."

"Oh, sure," Magill grinned, taking it as a joking compliment. But as the attorney eagerly launched into the history of the fabled mine, Magill realized he was quite serious.

He was surprised to find that he still recalled the main outlines of the story, of how in the 1840s the Peralta family had ventured north from their rancho in Sonora, Mexico, to find the fabulously rich lode; of how on the return from one such trip, just as they were leaving the mountains to cross the desert, they had been trapped in a canyon and, to a man, massacred by the Apaches; of how two prospectors, the Dutchman and his partner, the carpenter Jacob Wiser, had saved the life of a Peralta descendant in a cantina brawl and in gratitude had been given a map to the mine; of how when they found it, it proved to be richer by far than anticipated, the gold so loose they could scoop it up with their hands; and of how the Dutchman had then killed his partner and a score of others to protect his secret.

There were many clues to the mine's whereabouts, the attorney explained. On his deathbed the Dutchman had carefully described the mine to his mistress, the mulatto Julia Thomas, omitting only its exact location. But the most important clue, he was convinced, was not left by the Dutchman, but by one of the Peralta descendants.

Suddenly Magill found himself listening attentively. He was unfamiliar with this part of the tale.

In the 1870s, at the same time the Dutchman was working the mine, one Ramón Peralta y Gonzales, following the deathbed instructions of his father-in-law, had gone north from Sonora into Arizona Territory, in search of his family's hereditary mine. He carried a rough map marked with the mine's location. Its most important clue referred to Cañon Fresco—a "fresh canyon" located somewhere in the Superstition range. It was here, in an oasis of grass, water, and shade, that the Peraltas had hobbled their mules, very close to the mine.

Ramón had found neither the canyon nor the mine. Enroute, he had stumbled instead upon the site where the Peralta massacre had occurred some years earlier. And here, among the sun-bleached skeletons of his relatives, he had found a number of rotting saddlebags. The fortune in gold concentrates contained there was apparently more than enough wealth for Ramón, who returned to Mexico, along with his map, not to be heard of again.

Magill recalled some of the things he had read about the Superstitions. Although located only 40 miles from Phoenix, they were considered one of the most desolate and forbidding areas on the North American continent. They were not mountains in any ordinary sense, but sheer bluffs of ill-formed rock rising sharply from the desert floor. "If there were such a place in that area as a 'fresh canyon,' with abundant water and grass, you'd think that someone would certainly have found it before this," Magill interjected. "From what I remember reading about these mountains, there couldn't be many places that fit that description."

"That's just it, Glenn," the attorney replied excitedly. "There aren't any. And no one has ever found it. But so far everyone has always looked for it from the ground, by packing in. Remember, however, that the Dutchman described his mine as being on the side of a mountain. I think Cañón Fresco is hidden away on top of one of those mountains! That's why I believe that using modern methods—particularly a helicopter —we could find it.

"Would you be willing to go into partnership with me?" he asked abruptly. "I'll raise the money and you conduct the investigation."

The blunt offer caught Magill off guard. "Even if we found

the canyon, it might take months, even years, to locate the mine itself—assuming there is such a mine."

"You find the canyon and it doesn't matter how long it takes. I'll worry about the money. I know half a dozen men who will beg me to buy in, once they hear about it. What do you say?"

"I'll have to think about it," Magill answered. There were, he knew, many private detectives who would jump at such an offer. One friend, with an agency in San Francisco, had spent eight years on a single case that took him all over Europe. Of such things were investigators' dreams made. But Magill was not enthusiastic. He promised to think about it only because the attorney was a client who had just paid him a sizable fee and who, due to the nature of his business, could be counted on for similar assignments in the future.

"As soon as I get back to Denver," the attorney said, "I'll send you all the material I have on the mine. All I ask is that you look it over and let me know, honestly, what you think."

Magill nodded agreement.

"It's funny," he told his wife, Melba, after the attorney left them at their hotel. "During the couple of months I was on this case I developed a respect for that man. He showed good business sense. He didn't try to tell me how to do my job. He didn't expect miracles overnight. And in just a few minutes it's all disappeared."

"You don't believe there is such a mine?" she asked.

"I wouldn't be too surprised," he replied, "if the Dutchman himself had never existed."

On his return to Oklahoma City, Magill quickly forgot the conversation. Although there were several investigators in his employ, a backlog of cases had built up during his absence. There was an employee theft case (cashiers to be watched and checked out); a bar owner who suspected his waitresses of providing customers with extracurricular services; an out-of-state school principal suspected of molesting young boys; several cases requiring round-the-clock surveillance; and the usual round of husbands' having their wives watched and wives' monitoring their husbands' activities (the latter usually outnumbered the former about 10 to 1). Too, Christmas was approaching. Most missing-persons cases are seasonal. Children most often run away during the late spring and early summer, husbands during the holidays.

When the attorney's information arrived, he scanned it and then tossed it on top of a filing cabinet.

Nearly two months later, when a letter from the attorney arrived, it joined the package. Though he intended to answer, even the intention was soon forgotten.

A second letter was followed by a telephone call from Denver.

Had he had a chance to look over the material?

No, Magill frankly admitted, he hadn't. He'd been too busy. He promised to do so soon, however.

Late that night he made time. It was just about what he had expected, several dozen magazine articles and newspaper clippings relating to the story of the mine.

Magill read every word, less out of real interest than habit. Having worked as an accountant, then as a "bond buster" for a business investigative survey company, from which he had gone on to obtain his license and open his own detective agency, he was aware of the importance of detail.

On finishing the last article he was more than ever convinced that the story was a complete fabrication. The accounts contradicted one another on practically every point, from the Dutchman's name (given variously as Jacob Walz, Walsz, Waltz, Walzer, and von Walzer) to the number of men he had personally killed (from two to over a hundred) and to the amount of gold he had taken from his mine (from a low of a quarter million to 160 times that).

He could point out these discrepancies. But if the attorney was really suffering from "gold fever," as he certainly appeared to be, he had probably already noticed and chosen to overlook them. Facts never bothered a confirmed treasure seeker.

The easiest way to get the man off his back, he decided, would be to disprove the existence of the Dutchman. It was always easier to prove a positive than a negative, yet if he could tell him that after a thorough search of all available records he could find no documented proof that the legendary miner had ever existed, the attorney would at least have to discard the partnership idea. Magill decided that as soon as the opportunity presented itself he would go to Phoenix.

It came sooner than expected, due to the philandering of a Tulsa oilman. Late one night he received a long-distance call. The voice was female, the tone so familiar he could guess what she would say before she said it. Her husband was leaving that weekend to attend a convention in Phoenix. Oddly enough, his secretary was going on vacation at the same time. The wife had more than enough evidence to suspect that the two trips were related, but had to be sure.

Magill explained that his agency had affiliates throughout the United States and abroad as well, and that he could easily arrange for a Phoenix agency to keep the man under surveillance.

The woman insisted he handle the assignment himself.

Magill flew to Phoenix. Since the oilman was attending meetings mornings and afternoons, and his wife was primarily interested in his nighttime activities, Magill found himself with days free.

Where did one start a search for a legendary person?

In conventional cases, one began with a number of already established facts. In the Dutchman's case, however, this wasn't possible. What he needed was a fixed starting point from which to branch out. There was one thing on which a majority of accounts agreed: the date and circumstances of the Dutchman's death. This seemed as good a beginning as any.

Considering all the bloodshed attached to his legend, the Dutchman's reputed death had been most unromantic. Having stopped working the mine sometime after the death of his partner, supposedly from fear of the Apaches, the Dutchman had bought a parcel of land outside Phoenix and settled down to raising chickens. His acreage was right beside the Salt River, however, and when in February, 1891, the Salt overflowed its banks, inundating Phoenix, the Dutchman had been forced to take refuge in a tree. Finally rescued after considerable exposure, he was taken to the residence of his long-time friend, the mulatto Julia Thomas, who tried to nurse him through his pneumonia. He died the following October, but not before describing the mine to her and telling her that under the fireplace in his cabin was buried some $1,200 in gold, subsequently recovered.

Early his first morning in Phoenix, Magill went to the Arizona State Department of Library and Archives, located on the third floor of the State Capitol, and asked to see any newspapers for October, 1891. He was given microfilms of the *Phoenix Daily Herald* and was most of the way through the month when, in the issue for Monday, the 26th, he turned to the third page, where a name at the bottom of the first column caught his eye.

The item was brief. Yet, despite his conviction that the Dutchman story was probably a myth, he couldn't help but feel excited.

> Jacob Waltz, aged 81 years, died at 6 A.M. Sunday, October 25, 1891, and was buried at 10 o'clock this morning, from the residence of Mrs. J. E. Thomas, who had kindly nursed him through his last illness. Deceased was a native of Germany and spent the last thirty years of his life in Arizona, mining part of the time, ranching and raising chickens. His honest, industrious, amiable

character led Mrs. Thomas to care for him during his final days on earth, and he died with a blessing for her on his lips.

Hardly the description of a gold-crazed murderer!

Magill asked the librarian if she had any other Phoenix papers for the same date. She brought him the *Arizona Daily Gazette.* In the issue of Tuesday, October 27th, he found another obituary, briefer but with the same facts. In both accounts the name was spelled "Waltz."

> Jacob Waltz died Sunday evening at the residence of Mrs. J. E. Thomas and was buried yesterday. Deceased was a native of Germany and was 81 years old.

Magill now went back to the papers for the previous February, searching for some mention of Waltz in the flood stories. In the Friday, February 20th, issue of the *Herald,* he found what he was looking for. According to the news item, about 9 P.M. the previous night, Ed Scarborough and Henry King had set out in a boat to rescue people marooned by the waters. Southeast of town, they found three men on the roof of Jake Star's home. While this building had withstood the raging torrent, others located nearby had been less fortunate: "several abodes, not having been embanked, fell including those of Beckett, Pesquiera, butcher Gryalba, Jake Walts, one belonging to four Swedes and two Mexican houses back of Starr's."

Magill now had two possible names—Waltz and Walts. A brief reading of the *Herald,* however, indicated that its editor had a rather informal, phonetic approach to spelling. Star, for example, was rendered in the same account with both a single and a double "r."

He returned to his notes on the obituary. Waltz had come to Arizona 30 years previous to 1891. He asked the librarian what she had in the way of city records for about 1860.

"Nothing," she laughed. "Phoenix didn't come into existence

until 1868." However, she added, in April, 1864, the governor, hoping to have Arizona changed from territorial status to statehood, had ordered a census. This was available on microfilm, if he was interested.

Magill was. But he was not particularly hopeful. In the West, in those days, many men were not anxious to give their names and occupations to officials, be they sheriffs or census takers. Too, although the various accounts did not place the Dutchman in the Superstitions much before the 1870s, it was possible that he had been there earlier. And Magill could hardly picture a census taker trekking in, fighting off Apaches en route, just to ask a few questions.

In 1864 the Territory of Arizona claimed 4,187 inhabitants, not counting Indians. Magill began to scan the lists of names. There were a few quaint entries—such as the appellation "mistress" behind quite a few female names. He was in the last section, covering the Third District, Yavapai County, which took in Prescott and Wickenburg, where most mining activity of that time was centered, when he spotted it.

> Jacob Waltz, age 54, single male, born in Germany, resident in Arizona two years, naturalized citizen——

(To prove naturalization, a man had to "show papers." Magill wished he could have been peeping over the census taker's shoulder when Waltz showed his.)

> ——occupation miner, value of real estate and personal estate——

These last two columns were blank. Apparently Waltz had declined to state his net worth.

Having pinpointed Waltz's arrival date in Arizona as 1862 and his death date as 1891, Magill began to fill in the gap. He drew blanks in most of his sources: city and business directories for Phoenix, Tucson, and Prescott contained no mention of Waltz, though there was considerable information in Phoenix listings about the woman known as Mrs. J. E., or Julia, Thomas. There were a number of ads for her ice-cream parlor and candy shop, also for her boarding house on Washington Street.

He found Waltz again in 1876, in the Great Register for Maricopa County, where Phoenix was located: Jacob Waltz, age sixty-six. In the U.S. Census for 1880, Waltz, age seventy, was listed as living in Phoenix, place of birth Prussia, place of birth of mother and father, Prussia, occupation farmer! In 1882, age seventy-two, he was mentioned in the Maricopa Register again, and again in 1886, age seventy-six—only this time there was an additional nugget—and, for Magill's purpose, one more precious than gold. The listing further stated that Waltz had been naturalized as an American citizen at Los Angeles, California, in the Court for the First District, on July 19, 1861. By following this vein through Immigration and Naturalization, he should be able——

"I'm sorry, sir. We close at five."

He had been so intent on his search that he hadn't noticed the time. He hadn't even been out to lunch.

Sipping Jack Daniels and water in the bar of the Arizona Biltmore, Magill found it hard to dismiss Jacob Waltz from his thoughts. Due to the nature of his business, often having to work on a number of cases at the same time, he had of necessity developed the ability to turn off one and immediately switch his full attention to another. He now found it necessary to remind himself that he was not being paid to look for the Dutchman.

She was a tall brunette, much younger and much prettier than the snapshot indicated. He, on the other hand, was just about what Magill had been told to expect: a pompous braggart who talked too loud, berated the bartender, and had to top everyone else's story with a better one of his own. Magill had no trouble getting the seat next to him; even the other conventioneers found him insufferable.

On more than a few cases, Magill had found that his personal sympathies were less with his client than with the person he was investigating. This was particularly true in many missing-spouse cases—causing him to wonder not why the husband had run away but how he had managed to stay with his mate for any length of time. In this case there were no such reservations.

Things were far easier than he had expected. Earlier, for five dollars, a bellhop had supplied him with a delegate badge; another five now bought a round of drinks, which ripened the new friendship and led to further drinks in the oilman's suite, from his "private stock."

"She's not really my wife, you know," the middle-aged speculator drunkenly admitted in the early hours of the morning, roughly pulling the brunette onto his lap and pinching her so hard she winced. "Pretty nice piece for such an old boy, don't you think?" Magill had to agree, while the miniature transmitter in his shirt pocket relayed the conversation to the tape recorder in the back of the rental car in the hotel parking lot.

During the next three days Magill continued his research on the Dutchman. It is probable that the private detective is one of the few persons who really appreciates modern governmental bureaucracy. Today it is all but impossible for a man to "disappear"; through the need for a driver's license, Social Security number, draft card, Blue Cross, medical records, military service records, income tax returns, credit cards, he leaves a paper trail wherever he goes. In the Dutchman's time, however, such records were few. And a great many of them hadn't survived the passage of time or were stored away in some forgotten place. Visiting several city and state offices, Magill searched through stacks of paper—property records, deeds, mining claims, police records, marriage licenses, adding bits and pieces to his knowledge of the man Jacob Waltz.

On the last day of the convention, the oilman and his secretary flew back to Tulsa on separate planes. The report had already preceded them. As with many of his cases, Magill never learned the outcome. It was one of the minor frustrations, and blessings, of his profession. He did know, however, that if this was a typical case, the report would probably never see the inside of a divorce court. Some wives used such information to blackmail their husbands. Most, however, just had to know. In probably eight cases out of ten, the husbands were never told they had been under surveillance. Suspicion and uncertainty were the worst things, client after client had told Magill. "I had to know to set my mind at rest." He had heard the same phrase dozens of times, both in cases where investigation confirmed initial suspicions and in those—no small number—where doubt was proven unfounded.

When Magill returned to Oklahoma City he carried with him the skeleton of a man's life, plus more than a dozen leads for further investigation.

The "Dutchman" had existed. He was not Dutch, but German, and his name was not Walz, Walts, or von Walzer, but Waltz.

This did not mean Jacob Waltz ever had a mine, however.

CHAPTER 2

In Search of Cañón Fresco

WHAT the private-eye stories on TV do not mention about an investigator's life is the dull, mundane detail: the dozens of leads whose falseness is apparent only after they are patiently and completely checked out, the bright hopes that suddenly dissolve.

And the long waits.

Magill wrote letters: to Immigration and Naturalization, attempting to learn more of Jacob Waltz's past; to Wells Fargo, the National Archives, and the United States Mint, hoping to document the Dutchman's ore shipments; to the County Clerk of Los Angeles County, California, to verify Waltz's citizenship. To check out the history of the Peralta family, he wrote not only to Catholic archivists in Mexico and Spain but also to the Church of Jesus Christ of Latter-Day Saints in Salt Lake City, since the Mormons maintain one of the largest genealogical libraries in the world.

The replies were slow in coming back. Until they did, Magill didn't consider the information he had worth reporting to the attorney. Jacob Waltz remained a lifeless skeleton, composed of bare facts, devoid of details.

What he needed most was more firsthand information. It occurred to him that since Waltz hadn't died until 1891, there might be people still living who remembered him. Going back through the stories, now grown to a sizable number, he selected the most important names and started a background check on each.

Julia Thomas had died in 1917. During her last years she had turned the Dutchman myth to profit: for a small price she would talk to anyone, and for seven dollars more she would throw in a map guaranteed to lead straight to the mine, an interesting development, considering an article that had appeared in the *Arizona Weekly Gazette* of September 1, 1893:

> A QUEER QUEST
> Another "Lost Mine" Being
> Hunted for by a Woman
>
> Mrs. E. W. Thomas, formerly of the Thomas' ice cream parlors, is now in the Superstition Mountains engaged in a work usually deemed strange to woman's sphere. She is prospecting for a lost mine, to the location of which she believes she holds the key. But somehow, she has failed, after two months work to locate the bonanza, though aided by two men. The story of the mine is founded upon the usual death-bed revelations of the ancient miner usual in such cases. There is also a lost cabin connected with it. Its location is supposed to be a short distance from the western end of the main Superstition Mountain.

Julia Thomas not only failed to find the mine, but as her mind grew less than clear, the Dutchman's instructions to her underwent frequent modifications. This created a very special problem, since the major clues to the location of the site were in these last words. Which of her many versions was the most accurate?

One other person had been present during this important conversation, Reiney Petrasch, a young man who sometimes ran errands for Mrs. Thomas. It was Reiney she had sent to Waltz's adobe to recover the gold beneath the hearth, and he and his brother, Hermann, were the two men who had accompanied her on her unsuccessful expedition. Reiney had committed suicide in Globe in 1943. Failing memory had altered his recollections also, although in earlier accounts they agreed substantially with those of Julia Thomas.

Reiney's brother, Hermann Petrasch, had died in Superior a decade later. Over the years he told a number of people he had known the Dutchman personally; however, in an article that appeared in *Desert Magazine* he admitted that he had never met the man. He had come to Arizona only after the Dutchman's death, at the request of Reiney, to help in the search.

Some dozen others who had either known the Dutchman or had figured prominently in some latter aspect of the story were all dead. Among them was W. A. "Tex" Barkley, owner of the Circle-Quarter-U Ranch, located at the edge of the Superstitions. Barkley had led many sheriff's posses in search of people who disappeared in the mountains. Although he had not known the Dutchman, as a young girl his wife, Gertrude, had. The account of Barkley's death, some years earlier, mentioned he was survived by his widow. Magill doubted that she was still living, but he ran a telephone check and found she still resided on a portion of the old ranch.

He called her.

No, she couldn't help him, she said. She was an old lady, totally blind, living with only a nurse for companion. She was sure she could add nothing to what he already knew.

Was it true she had known the Dutchman?

Yes. As a little girl she had often seen him on the streets of

Phoenix, with his burros, returning from or going to the Superstitions. But, she added, "You wouldn't want to come all the way to Arizona just to talk to an old lady."

Magill assured her there was nothing he would rather do. If he made the trip, would she let him call on her?

Perhaps, she replied. But on one condition: that he wouldn't ask her any questions about the murder of Adolph Ruth.

Magill gave her a qualified answer: he assured her she wouldn't have to tell him anything she didn't want to.

Since he had started his investigation, Magill had been strongly tempted to look into the various Superstition murders and disappearances. Adolph Ruth's demise—he was first shot, then beheaded—was just one of an impressive number of strange deaths that had occurred during the past three decades. Why so many? Was there a pattern in the killings? (Ruth was not the only one to be beheaded.) Was—as some people claimed—a single person, or group of persons, responsible?

Fascinating as these mysterious murders could prove to be, Magill decided to avoid investigating them for the time being. He was already aware of how easily the search could turn into a full-time occupation. Moreover, he had troubles enough already. There was, for example, the problem of overlapping myths—particularly, the story of Geronimo's treasure cave.

In studying the legends and lore of the various Indian tribes inhabiting Arizona, W. Irven Lively* noticed a curious thing. All had a common attitude toward the mountains the white men called the Superstitions: each believed they were the abode of Evil Spirits.

The Pimas and Maricopas who lived in the Salt River Valley avoided the mountains, believing that to enter them meant im-

* *The Mystic Mountains,* by W. Irven Lively, privately printed by the author, Phoenix, 1955.

mediate death. According to one Pima legend, when the Spanish first began their conquest of the New World, Montezuma gathered together his people and brought them to the Superstitions. There they had dwelt ever since, in the heart of the mountains, behind a magic stone gateway, awaiting the day they would come forth and repossess the land. To invade their sanctuary brought instant retribution.

The attitude of the Apaches was more complex. To them, the Wee-Kit-Sour-Ah, the "Rocks Standing Up," were the home of the Thunder Gods, the place where storms were born. In Apache cosmology, these volcanic outcroppings performed a special function, serving as a kind of purgatory through which each Apache soul had to pass after death. They too believed the spirits evil, and feared them. But the Apaches were practical as well as religious. These particular mountains were a natural fortress from which they could pour forth to raid and in which they could easily hide if pursued. Instead of avoiding the spirits, they placated them by designating one portion of the mountains sacred. Even today, those Apaches who still cling to the old ways are not willing to divulge just which part. In some of their legends, the sacred place is a ceremonial cave, in others a never clearly identified section of the mountains.

Some modern searchers after the myth guess the area to be on the mountain known as Geronimo's Head. Others place it in Needle Canyon, within sight of the peak known as Weaver's Needle. And some believe the area and Geronimo's treasure cave to be one and the same.

At the turn of the century, while a captive at Fort Sill, Oklahoma, Geronimo offered one of his guards "one million dollars in white man's gold" to help him escape. Dubiously, the guard asked Geronimo where he could get that kind of money. From his treasure cave in the Superstitions, Geronimo told him. It was here, Geronimo said, that he often hid from the soldiers.

"From my cave," he was quoted as saying, "I can see the soldiers on the military trail below, but they can't see me."

Although the guard was tempted, the plot was exposed. Contemptuously, Geronimo declared they needn't try to find the cave without him. It was too well hidden. He could give them clues and still they would never find it. There was a spring at the foot of a mountain, in a deep canyon. If you followed the water to its source, high up in a sunken valley, there the cave would be.

The cave was never found. Nor did Geronimo ever return to it. In 1909, after a drunken night in town, he caught a wagon back to the fort, fell off, and lay unnoticed by the roadside in freezing temperatures. He died of pneumonia several days later.

Checking out the tale, Magill called the archivist at Fort Sill, who confirmed the story of the attempted bribery. But Geronimo had been a notorious liar, he reminded Magill, lying not only to white men, but also to his own people.

Magill contacted the Apache Council at Warm Springs, New Mexico, and asked whether any members of Geronimo's family were still living. His son, Robert, was, Magill was told, at Mescalero, New Mexico. However, Robert Geronimo had never known his father; he had been born on the Mescalero Apache reservation in 1889, shortly after his father was taken prisoner. A better source was John Goochie, a member of Geronimo's old band who was now living in Apache, Oklahoma.

On his first free day Magill drove there. Although many of the Indians in this area were comparatively well off, from oil monies, Goochie, with his large family, was living in extreme poverty in a shack just outside town.

It was impossible to determine his age. His grandchildren, who were as old as Magill, knew only that he was over 100. He was a short, dark, extremely wrinkled man, still dressed in the old style, with long braided hair, once-blue denim pants that bore no evidence of ever having been washed, and well-worn cowboy boots.

"You come to hear about Geronimo," Goochie anticipated. Magill admitted that he had. Motioning for him to squat down on the ground and listen, Goochie recited, as if by rote, the story of Geronimo's raids, his four surrenders, and of how, following the last, he and all the Chiricahuas—most of whom had taken no part in the raids—had been transported to Florida, to live in captivity. "Like pigs, pigs and cattle, they treated us. Only not so good. Animals get to breed. They separated us from our wives so we could not make more Apaches."

From Florida they had been taken to Alabama, then to Fort Sill, and eventually all, except Geronimo, were allowed to move onto reservations. The citizens of Arizona had put pressure on the President and Congress to keep the old warrior imprisoned, for fear he would try to return to his former hunting grounds.

When Goochie paused for breath, Magill asked him about the escape attempt.

Goochie remained silent a moment, then his eyes sparkled with recollection. Yes, he remembered. The white man had actually believed that if he let Geronimo escape he would show him to his treasure cave. Goochie roared in amusement at this. "Geronimo was a liar. He lied to General Crook. He lied to his own people."

"Then you don't think he had such a cave?" Magill asked.

"Oh, he had treasure cave all right," Goochie asserted. As a boy he had heard about it. The cave was in the Wee-Kit-Sour-Ah, in a sacred place, by a hidden valley, near water. The water fell over the face of the mountain.

"A waterfall, you mean?"

Goochie nodded. If you followed the water to its source, back behind the falls, there was the cave. Many, many moons ago, Goochie continued, animated by the memory, he and a group of other young braves had decided to lure the secret of the cave from Geronimo, then go there and take out the treasure. Though they knew the cave was in a sacred place, they were young and foolish. They used various artifices to win Geronimo's confidence—flattering him, giving him presents. But old and tired though he was, he was craftier than they. After taking their presents, he called them together and threatened to kill them all should even a single one go in search of the cave.

Geronimo was a bad liar, Goochie repeated, but this time they believed him.

"Are you going to look for the cave?" Goochie asked.

"Perhaps," Magill replied.

"Take me with you."

For a long moment Magill paused, not knowing what to say.

Looking around him, at his children and grandchildren, it was Goochie who finally broke the silence. "No, soon enough I'll be making that journey."

John Goochie, whose years spanned a century, was another of Coronado's Children.

By now, Magill's research had developed into a pattern. If a story seemed even remotely possible, he would investigate it, in hope of disproving it. Once disproven, it could be discarded and something else tackled.

For example, one account stated that the Dutchman and his partner, Jacob Wiser, had served together in the Confederate Army. From his research in the Arizona State Library, Magill had documented proof that Waltz had been in Arizona in 1862, 1864, and 1876. Chronologically, the story was possible. A check of the National Archives, however, failed to turn up service records on either man.

Rather than being discouraged, he came to welcome such blind leads. As, item by item, he eliminated possibilities, he could concentrate on others more promising.

There were at least two good reasons for dismissing the Geronimo treasure cave as a probable myth. One was Geronimo's known fondness for fabrication. Another was that on one occasion the colorful chief had placed his cave in the Sierra Madre, on still another in the Guadalupes.

And yet Magill couldn't entirely eliminate it from consideration. The Peralta tale had mentioned a hidden valley with abundant water. Geronimo had described his cave as being similarly located. According to his guard at Fort Sill, Geronimo had bragged, "From my cave, I can see the soldiers on the military trail below, but they can't see me." Jacob Waltz, in describing his mine to Julia Thomas, was quoted as saying, "From the mouth of my mine I can look down and see people on the old military trail. But they can't see my mine."

In his research thus far, Magill had set up two categories: those matters established to his own satisfaction, and those he had disproven. To these he now added a third—things he could neither prove nor disprove, things that warranted further investigation.

Reluctantly, he had to place the Geronimo story in this last category.

Although Magill had first contacted Mrs. Barkley in the summer of 1964, it was fall before his work load permitted him to consider going to Arizona. Magill and his family habitually spent the Christmas holidays with his wife's family in Albuquerque, New Mexico, halfway between Oklahoma City and Phoenix. Although he used the visit to Mrs. Barkley as justification for the trip, he ultimately had to admit to himself another, stronger reason: he was anxious to go into the Superstitions.

Shortly after arriving in Albuquerque, he went to the public library, looking for two books on the Superstitions that he had thus far not been able to get: *The Lost Dutchman*, by Sims

Ely, and *Thunder God's Gold*, by Barry Storm. He was again unsuccessful, but the librarian remembered that some years earlier a local newspaperman, Robert Crandall, had written a series of articles on the Superstition Mountains. By her recollection, Crandall had spent a number of years there, searching for treasure of some sort. She didn't know, however, whether Crandall was still living in Albuquerque. The paper he had worked for was now defunct and could be of no help in tracing him.

On an off chance, Magill checked the Albuquerque phone directory, which listed two Robert Crandalls. He connected with the first call. Crandall was quite willing to talk to him; in fact, he strongly recommended their meeting before Magill's first trip into the Superstitions; he could offer a few pointers that just might save his life. They arranged to meet the following afternoon. To Magill's surprise, Crandall's house was located directly behind that of his wife's relatives.

For some reason Magill had expected an elderly man. Instead Robert Crandall was his own age, in his late thirties, a tall, dark-haired, handsome man who now made his living as a commercial photographer.

"I understand you've spent a good bit of time looking for the Lost Dutchman Mine," Magill commented by way of openers.

"Not five minutes," Crandall replied. "I've spent about ten years in those mountains all right, but I was looking for the Jesuit priests' treasure.

"*For what?*" To date, this made the third treasure legend placed within the confines of the Superstitions.

Crandall filled him in on the tale.

For all their vows of poverty, the Jesuits were a wealthy order, he explained. Within a few decades after their arrival in the New World, they had amassed a great fortune from the gold and silver mines of northern Mexico and southern Arizona. They had not declared most of their wealth, however, even though by law the King of Spain was entitled to one-fifth. This, at least, was one of the charges King Carlos III made against them in 1767, when he ordered the expulsion of the Jesuits from all Spanish lands.

Shortly before this, however, anticipating just such a development, the Jesuit priests had gathered up all records and church treasures of the eighteen missions that lay between Sonora and Casa Grande. These included reliquaries, chalices, censors, candelabra, many of solid gold, many the product of their richest mines, which were located in the Sierra Madre and the Superstitions. It was to the Superstitions that they decided to return them for safekeeping. According to legend, after their trek to the missions the priests had been seen entering the Superstitions from the south, with 240 heavily loaded jacks. Later, when they emerged from the mountains, near the site of what later became Fort McDowell, the mules no longer had their burdens. Legend had it that the treasure had been buried on, or in the vicinity of, Weaver's Needle, the large peak that also played a prominent part in the Dutchman's story.*

Crandall showed Magill an old map on which the eighteen missions were depicted. The northernmost was only a few miles from the Superstition Mountains.

Magill listened politely but asked few questions. He was not ready to believe in the Dutchman's lost gold, much less still in another treasure trove.

From his own personal knowledge, Crandall said, he could attribute three deaths to the Jesuit priests' treasure.

Early in the 1950s he and an old prospector, Ed Piper, had

* For more information on the Jesuit priests' treasure, see *Apache Gold and Yaqui Silver*, by J. Frank Dobie, Little Brown, New York, 1950; *1001 Lost, Buried or Sunken Treasures*, by F. L. Coffman, Thomas Nelson & Sons, New York, 1957; and *Treasures of the World*, by Robert Charroux, Paul S. Ericksson, Inc., New York, 1966.

formed a partnership to look for the Jesuit riches. They were not alone in their search, however. Several years earlier Celeste Marie Jones appeared in the mountains, where she staked out Weaver's Needle as her own special domain.

Celeste Jones, who claimed to be a former star of the Metropolitan Opera, was a gigantic Negro woman with a penchant for tight-fitting, gold-colored Bermuda shorts. The leader of a Southern California cult, she financed her well-equipped expeditions into the Superstitions through a sort of holy lottery, each convert being entitled to one share of the treasure—when found—for each dollar contributed. She was not searching for the Lost Dutchman Mine (she claimed to have found this as early as 1950), but for the Jesuit stash, to whose location she had fourteen symbolical clues, one an alabaster cross atop Weaver's Needle.

In 1959 she reappeared in the Superstitions, accompanied by a large, well-armed party. With a huge charge of dynamite, she blasted away the cross, declaring that she would level 4,535-foot Weaver's Needle stone by stone, if necessary, to unearth the treasure. Trouble between the Jones and Piper camps broke out almost immediately, Mrs. Jones taking a number of potshots at the Piper crew with her favorite .30-06 as they worked down the mountain.

In retaliation Piper quietly invaded Mrs. Jones' camp one night and stole her arsenal. Mrs. Jones brought charges against Piper, Piper against Mrs. Jones. Judge Norman Teason, of Apache Junction, confiscated all the long-range weapons of both groups—apparently operating on the theory that if a man was to be shot he at least had the right to be close enough to see his assailant.

On Armistice Day, 1959, as Crandall and Piper were en route to their diggings, Robert St. Marie, a twenty-two-year-old ex-paratrooper employed by Mrs. Jones as a gunman-companion, stepped out from behind a boulder with pistol in hand to inform them that Mrs. Jones had given him orders to shoot them if they set foot on the Needle.

Piper immediately dropped behind another boulder, drew his .357 magnum, and pumped three shots into St. Marie's guts.

In mid-November a coroner's jury ruled the killing justifiable self-defense.

Less than a week later, Vern Rowlee, one of Ed Piper's employees, went berserk in Needle Canyon. Confronting a pair of hikers, Ralph Thomas and his wife, he accused them of being FBI agents and tried to disarm Thomas. In the ensuing scuffle, Thomas' gun went off, shooting Rowlee in the stomach. Thomas was later acquitted of the killing.

In the Superstitions, Crandall remarked without a trace of a smile, people take their treasure hunting seriously.

One other death was accidental. One day he and Piper had come upon a man near death in one of the canyons. He had been hiking, he said, when he stumbled into a hole and broke his leg. On recovering consciousness, he had seen the figure of a priest standing before him. At first he had thought it was an hallucination but on looking closer discovered it was a statue, made entirely of gold. (Such a statue, life-size, not only fashioned of gold plate but filled with gold dust, was part of the Jesuit treasure tale.) The hole, the man had discovered, was in reality a large cave. With considerable effort, he had finally succeeded in extricating himself. But when Piper and Crandall questioned him about the cave's location, he lapsed into unconsciousness. He died the same night in a hospital in Florence, without recovering consciousness.

The stories were incredible. Yet, later, checking newspaper records, Magill verified all three.

"In there," Crandall warned him, "nature itself is against you."

There were, he said, three distinct species of rattlesnakes: the common, ordinary kind, down in the canyons; a sidewinder type that inhabited the mountains; and in the higher mountains, a short, stubby rattler that belied its name, since it struck without warning. There were also double-tailed scorpions whose sting would paralyze an arm or leg for days. There were mountain lion, bear, and javelina—wild pigs which would charge viciously if cornered, even accidentally.

There was heat. And water only at certain times of the year. And there was man.

You had to be prepared for all.

It was folly to go into the Superstitions alone, Crandall said. A sprained ankle or a broken leg meant death. But it was madness to go in with someone you didn't totally trust, as those mountains did something to a man's mind. He strongly advised Magill, before going in, to tell someone he could rely on the exact area he planned to explore and the exact date he was coming out; if he failed to appear, a sheriff's party could be sent in to search for him. He also told him the unwritten rules of the Superstitions.

Mind your own business.

The fewer people you tell your plans to, the safer you will be.

Leave your gun in your holster unless you intend to use it. In there, Crandall said, if you come around a trail and encounter a man with a gun in his hand, shoot first.

The two men talked all afternoon. Even though he considered the Jesuit treasure story pure bunk, Magill felt the time well spent.

"By the way," Crandall said with a grin as Magill was going out the door, "there are people who claim the legendary Seven Cities of Cibola are also located in the Superstitions."

In calling the Phoenix helicopter service, Magill heeded Crandall's advice, telling them only his probable arrival date and that he would need a plane for several hours on two separate days. He was told that a plane would be available on a day's notice and that the rate would be twenty-five dollars an hour.

Approaching the small town of Apache Junction along Highway 60–70, Magill saw the Superstition Mountains for the first time. There were several mountain ranges near Phoenix. He had thought the Superstitions would be similar. They weren't. They were unlike any mountains he had ever seen. There were no foothills, no warning. The outer palisades rose straight up from the desert floor, like a gigantic fortress. Even in the hot Arizona sunlight, there was something dark and mysterious about them. They seemed as ancient as time.

A white-limestone ridge ran along their tops. The Pima Indians had a legend about it. Far far back in time, a great flood had covered the land, all except the peaks of these mountains. When the water receded, the white ridge remained, the mark of the foam. On hearing this tale, the early Spanish explorers had called them Sierra de la Espuma, Mountains of the Foam. No one seemed to know for sure just when or from whom they had received their present name.

Above the white ridge were a number of tall, monumental rocks. These, again according to the Pimas, were Indians trapped by the flood and turned to stone, the silent sentinels of the mountains. From their vantage point they could see, night or day, when a stranger entered. Magill could almost make out their faces.

Stopping for lunch, he studied the mountains and tried to analyze his feelings about them. From all he had learned thus far, he should have feared them, or at the very least felt apprehensive. Yet neither was the case. There was an almost paternal quality about them, as if they could be harsh or kind, whichever the occasion demanded. He could understand why the Apaches had chosen to court their favor. It was easier that way.

The waitress noticed his intent stare.

"They kind of get to you, don't they?"

He admitted that they did. "How do *you* feel about them?" he asked her.

"They scare me to death," she flatly stated. "Some mornings when I come to work I look at them and get the feeling that they're hundreds of miles away. But then other days—honest to God—you look and they seem to have moved up closer during the night. And you get the feeling that some night, without any warning, when everyone is asleep, they're going to move in and swallow everybody up."

She shivered.

"I'll tell you this. As soon as I can find some man stupid enough to marry me, I'm going to move a hell of a long ways away from this place!"

After inquiring about accommodations, Magill decided to stay at King's Ranch Resort, located at the edge of the mountains only a short distance from the home of Mrs. Barkley. The owner of the resort, Dr. Allan Bane, welcomed him warmly.

In his business Magill had learned to keep his own counsel. Yet he liked Bane from the moment he met him and found it difficult to heed Crandall's advice.

With a certain inevitability the talk turned to the mountains. A retired naturopath whose typical meal consisted of goat's milk and venison, Bane looked the epitome of the hearty outdoorsman. Yet he admitted to Magill that although he had lived on the edge of the Superstitions for years, he had ventured into the interior only once. A friend had parked his car on the opposite end and he had hiked through. It had been enough to satisfy his curiosity. Over the years he had seen many people go into the mountains; when they came out they were never the same.

Before seeing Mrs. Barkley, Magill wanted to check the mining records in Florence, county seat of Pinal, in which the Superstitions were partially located. Bane had some business in Florence and offered to take Magill with him.

As they were getting into the car, Magill noticed an odd cloud formation over the Superstition palisades. It took the form of a dark warhead. Thinking of the Apache tale that this was the place where storms were born, he asked Bane about it. "That's strange," Bane remarked thoughtfully. "In all the years I've lived here, I've never seen anything like that before."

Bane appeared disturbed by the sight.

As they drove away from the ranch, Magill looked back. The cloud had moved off the palisades and seemed to be traveling in their direction. By the time they reached Florence, neither he nor Bane was speaking. Neither wanted to voice his feelings. All the way the strange cloud had followed them, turning when they turned, stopping when they stopped, maintaining the same position, a few miles behind them, as if watching and waiting.

Mrs. Barkley was a thoroughly charming woman. They had tea and made small talk for perhaps fifteen minutes before Magill finally was able to interject the topic of the Dutchman. At the mention, a frown crossed her face.

"Did you know him well?" Magill asked.

It was a trick question, although he was sure she was not aware of it.

"No, not well," she replied thoughtfully. "I was only a little girl. No, I don't suppose anyone knew him well, except perhaps Mrs. Thomas. You see, we'd heard talk about him. About what he was supposed to have done to people who tried to follow him into the mountains. No one ever knew if the things were true. But all the same, people gave him a wide berth. He was not the sort of person you wanted to strike up a friendship with."

If she had read his thoughts she couldn't have answered the question better. He would have been immediately suspicious if she had claimed to have been an intimate of the Dutchman.

"What did he look like?" Magill asked, realizing he had never seen a description of him.

"He was a small man, with a big white beard. We children used to call him 'Old Snowbeard.' He had two burros. I can't remember their names, but I knew them once. He was a slow-moving, deliberate sort of man. There was something lonely about him—perhaps 'solitary' would be a better word—at least that's how I recall him now."

For the first time Jacob Waltz came alive for Magill.

"I suppose you've heard that he took most of his gold back into the mountains?"

No, Magill admitted, he hadn't heard that.

Mrs. Barkley recalled some of the stories about him. Although he had cashed in a fortune in gold, he had spent very little of it, leading people to conclude that he had a cache somewhere in the mountains. There really wasn't much you could spend money on in Phoenix in those days, she observed. Some said he had a weakness for beer and spent much of his time in the saloons on Washington Street. But beer was only a nickel a glass, and there was—she remembered peeking in as she went by—a huge free lunch.

She recalled other stories about him, but clearly identified them as second or third hand. She did know a number of old-timers who had known, or at least who claimed to have known, him. She'd be glad to give him their names.

She talked freely about the history of the lost mine, with a single exception—the murder of Adolph Ruth. Several weeks earlier, she said, Erle Stanley Gardner had visited her, asking if she would permit him to write the story of her life. She had refused, declaring there were things she knew that, if told, would make her fear for her life. She wasn't afraid of the mountains, she asserted, looking toward the picture window as if she could actually see them, though she was totally blind. What frightened her was the weird nature of some of the people who went into them.

It was only a guess, but Magill had the feeling that Mrs. Barkley knew—or believed she knew—who was responsible for Ruth's death, and that person was still living.

She brought out her scrapbook. It was a huge volume, filled with clippings, and at her sufferance Magill spent more than two hours reading them through. The articles were mostly on the murders and disappearances. He was surprised to find that the greatest number had occurred in recent years, that they dated almost to the time of his arrival. Tempted to question her further about them, he sensed that she had meant it when she had said she didn't want to discuss them.

Thanking her for her courtesy and apologizing for taking so much of her time, he rose to leave. She took his hand, squeezed it firmly, and said, "Promise me something."

"If I can."

"Don't go in there."

He hesitated.

"Oh, I know you will," she said. "Even though you didn't mention it, I knew it from your voice. But I had to try. I showed you that scrapbook for a reason, you know."

"I know," he replied.

Over the next several days, he interviewed some dozen old-timers mentioned by Dr. Bane and Mrs. Barkley and received the names and addresses of as many more who no longer lived in the vicinity.

Magill felt slightly out of his element questioning them. In the course of an ordinary investigation he could use many of the same tricks lawyers do: test questions, intensive cross-examination, badgering the witness into contradicting himself. Here, he had to proceed more gingerly.

His background aided him in other ways, however. There

was such a thing as a lying tone of voice. He could not define it, but he could recognize it. There were other telltale signs. When a person grew excited while telling a story it was usually the product of imagination. When sentences were preceded by "Believe me . . . ," "Take my word for it . . . ," or "You won't believe this . . ." he didn't.

Most of the stories he heard were second or third hand (some recited almost word-for-word articles they had read). One man said his father had been present on one occasion when the Dutchman cashed in ore. This had occurred in the mid-1870s, at Tucson, when the Dutchman sold two burro loads to Charlie Myers, an ore buyer, for $1,600. Two other men, whom he named, had been present when the sale took place. They had all examined the ore. It was in rose quartz and extremely rich. Asked where he got it, the Dutchman hadn't answered.

Another man didn't believe the Dutchman had a mine, but that he had been "high-grading" ore from the Vulture, a rich mine of the time and had "created" the Superstition mine as a cover for his thefts.

Bane also introduced Magill to a number of prospectors. One, who wore a .45 slung low on the hip, claimed to have found three of the old Peralta shafts. His mines were not in the Superstitions, however, but on their periphery, near the old-time boomtown of Goldfield. Like several others Magill talked to, he felt that the Peralta mines and the Dutchman's were entirely different workings (bringing to five the number of Superstition treasures to date). Magill asked whether he'd had any luck. The moment he asked he knew he'd broken some unwritten rule. The prospector's reply was an inaudible grunt.

Later Bane told Magill that the man had good reason for remaining silent. He was taking gold out of at least one of his shafts—Bane had seen it—and was bootlegging it to dentists in Phoenix. He also warned him to keep his distance if he encountered this man in the mountains. There was talk that he knew more than a little about some of the recent deaths. There was also speculation he was not using his real name. For years the Superstitions had been an area much favored by wanted men. It was territory into which the law was notably reluctant to venture. Two counties—Pinal and Maricopa—bisected the mountains; in the event of a killing, each sheriff played a game known locally as "It's your body."

Again and again Magill had to remind himself that this was the 1960s.

Following Crandall's advice, Magill purchased his supplies in Phoenix. He had already brought along two cameras—one movie, one still—and a .38 Police Special, which he sometimes found necessary to carry in his work.

Only a week of his vacation remained. He called the helicopter service to charter a plane for the following morning. On being asked where he wanted to go, he replied, "The Superstitions."

"You didn't tell us that when you called from Albuquerque."

"I didn't know it would make any difference."

"It makes a hell of a big difference," the man replied. "For one thing, that's damn rugged country, with treacherous downdrafts. You'll need a bigger craft, one equipped for any emergency that might arise—with compass facilities, spare parts, lots of water. Another thing, we also charge a higher rate to go there—fifty-five dollars an hour—and we can't set you down. That's part of the Tonto National Forest, a government wilderness area, and motorized vehicles aren't allowed in there."

Magill made no attempt to conceal his disappointment. He could pack in, but that way there would be no chance to look for Cañón Fresco. Not at all happy with the alternative, he arranged for the copter to pick him up at King's Ranch Resort the following morning. There was room for another passenger.

He asked Bane if he wanted to go along, and Bane eagerly said yes.

On lifting up over the palisades, the pilot told Magill that he didn't want to go in low over the mountains, that on several occasions he and the other pilots had been shot at. Magill angrily told him that he was being paid fifty-five dollars an hour to do exactly that, that he wanted to go in low and look at every mountain, valley, and canyon in the range.

Unhappily, the pilot nodded agreement.

Prior to the trip, Magill had spent hours studying photographs and a topographical map of the region. He knew all the statistics, that the highest peak, Superstition Mountain itself, was 5,057 feet, that the range covered 124,140 acres, nine times the land area of Manhattan Island. Yet the terrain was both far wilder and more varied than expected.

When they encountered no gunfire, the pilot relaxed a bit, pointing out the most prominent landmarks. He had heard many who claimed to have "explored" the Superstitions, he said, but most had never ventured off the government trail. Each spring the Dons Club of Phoenix held an annual encampment, staying out all night and telling ghost stories, but going only as far as Needle Canyon and never venturing into the really rugged interior. Even from the air, Magill could understand why.

One by one he identified the landmarks on the map: First Water, Fremont Pass, Geronimo's Head, La Barge, Boulder, and Needle Canyons. It was December, one of the few months when the waterholes were not dry, yet Magill saw nothing even vaguely resembling the Peralta clue.

Once they had covered the whole range, he asked the pilot to concentrate on the area around Weaver's Needle, the tall, blunt-shaped peak that served as key marker to all the treasure stories. This was also the general area where most of the deaths had taken place.

The pilot swooped down into Needle Canyon, low between two mountains, rising abruptly over the jagged cliffs of one. The movie camera had jammed, and Magill was trying to fix it, when out of the corner of his eye he thought he saw something. On the map the two mountains below were identified as Black Top and Bluff Springs. The latter was a wedge-shaped mountain surrounded by high, almost perpendicular cliffs. On Magill's instructions, the pilot circled and came back.

There, on the top of Bluff Springs Mountain, almost hidden even from air view, was a deep, recessed canyon, green with grass.

It had been so easy Magill was inclined to doubt his discovery. Only after flying over the whole range for more than an hour and seeing nothing else even vaguely resembling it did Magill become convinced that he had found Cañón Fresco.

On being set down outside Bane's home, Magill hurriedly made a call to Denver. Waiting for it to go through, he mentally rehearsed what he was going to say. "About that partnership . . . ," he thought he might begin.

Although trying to remain calm, he found it difficult to conceal his excitement.

The call was never completed. Magill spoke to the attorney's secretary. Just a week earlier, her employer had died unexpectedly of a heart attack.

CHAPTER 3

Seven Glittering Cities of Gold

DURING the next several months Magill tried to erase the Superstitions from his mind.

The death of the attorney had left him without a good reason to continue the investigation. He had neither the time nor the money for the detailed search required. Nor was there anyone to whom he could go for advice. On several occasions he had tried to broach the subject of the Lost Dutchman to friends. Their reaction had been predictable; a year or so ago he would have responded in precisely the same way. Grown men did not waste time on treasure hunts. He took his notes and shoved them into the back of a filing cabinet.

Yet, in the midst of a routine surveillance, an idea would occur to him. Mightn't Bluff Springs Mountain—which had a spring near its base, whose source was probably in the recessed valley atop the mountain—fit Geronimo's description?

At night he would often wake with other leads—a clue that

suddenly fit into place; a discrepancy that disproved, and thus eliminated, one of the accounts. And in the morning, when his wife arose, she would find him in his study, drawer of the filing cabinet open, photographs, maps, and articles spread out on his desk before him.

The more he tried to forget the stories, the deeper he pushed them into his subconscious, the more often he was reminded of them—with hunches, intuitive flashes.

Considering it logically, he realized the Lost Dutchman was becoming an obsession.

By now, much of his background research had been completed. Assembling his materials, he noticed two odd things about all the Superstition treasure legends. One was the common denominators, the similarities and parallels shared by each. The other was the strange way they dovetailed together in time.

The Seven Golden Cities of Cibola

One afternoon in the summer of 1536 four dirty, ragged men—three Spaniards and a Negro slave—stumbled into Mexico City, carrying with them a tale that would shape the history of the American Southwest.

The leader of the group was a Spaniard, Cabeza de Vaca; his arrival in the capital marked the end of an incredible eight-year ordeal. Originally part of a large group that had set out to explore the coasts of Florida, he and his party had lost contact with their ships and, fashioning their own crude craft, had set sail, landing near the present site of Galveston, Texas. From there they had walked across territory that would in time comprise three states—Texas, New Mexico, and Arizona—not only becoming the first Europeans to cross this portion of the North

American continent, but also the first to see buffalo, the first to encounter many of the Indian tribes.

Yet the inhabitants of Mexico City were far less interested in hearing of their privations, or their descriptions of the great, shaggy beasts, than in a rumor the travelers had heard from Indians en route: of seven glittering golden cities lying somewhere to the north of Mexico.

Although Cabeza de Vaca was unaware of it, the legend of the Seven Golden Cities had been ancient even in Montezuma's time.

Their story so excited the viceroy that an advance exploration party was dispatched. It was headed by a Franciscan friar, Marcos de Niza, who took along the Negro slave Esteban from the original party as his guide. As the group moved northward, the priest sent Esteban ahead to scout. If he found the cities and they were plain and poor, Esteban was to send back a cross the size of a man's hand. If they were large and wealthy, the cross should be twice that length. In the event their richness exceeded that of all Mexico, it was to be bigger still.

A messenger returned four days later, staggering under the weight of a cross as large as his body.

Fray Marcos hurried to catch up. Along the way, Indians told him the name of the cities: Cibola.

But meanwhile, Esteban had run into trouble. His fondness for Indian maidens and a propensity to lord it over the natives went unappreciated in some of the villages he passed through. While most villages yielded to his demand for tribute, one refused to take seriously his claim that an army of white men was following in his wake. Later a tribal chronicler would explain why they were sure he was lying: "It was nonsense for him to say that the people in the land whence he came were white, when he was black. . . ."

A messenger brought back word of Esteban's death.

Still, Fray Marcos pushed on, until he finally approached the first of the great cities. He did not actually enter, but from a nearby hill surveyed its eminence.

There have been many explanations as to what then happened, none of them satisfactory. Perhaps, some suggest, the priest was given to holy visions. Perhaps, like many other treasure hunters who would succeed him, he desired so badly to find the thing that he convinced himself he had done so. Or, as historian George P. Hammond has graciously put it, "Perhaps the sun shining on the houses made them glitter like gold and silver; perhaps the heat waves rising from the desert in a glorious mirage magnified the size of the town."

For when the priest returned to Mexico, he reported that it was a large city, much larger than Mexico City itself, its houses all made of stone, some ten stories high, and "there is much gold there and that the natives make it into vessels and jewels for their ears, and into little blades with which they wipe away their sweat." *

The expedition then formed was one of the greatest ever assembled on the continent. There were 300 Spaniards, the majority of noble lineage, "the flavor of the aristocracy"; there were 1,000 Indians, 1,000 horses, herds of sheep and swine, swivel guns and harquebuses. Although Hernando Cortes and Hernando de Soto fought to head it, the honor, after much politicking, went to young Francisco Vásquez de Coronado.

They encountered Indians almost immediately. Some, probably frightened by seeing horses for the first time, proved submissive. The rest did not. Disease, rough terrain, high mountains, burning desert and lack of food claimed many of the

* Generally overlooked is another part of his account, in which he stated that the gold was not native to this region, but had been obtained from the Painted Ones, in return for turquoises. As a sidelight, for what it is worth, the Painted Ones were the Pimas, and it was in their domain that the Superstition Mountains were located.

lives not taken by Indians. The "flavor of the aristocracy" had for the most part spent their lives in the soft comforts of cities. They died quickly.

Finally, however, much reduced in numbers, on July 7, 1540, they reached the first of the cities. Castañeda, official historian of the expedition, described what happened: "When they saw the first village, which was Cibola, such were the curses that some hurled at Friar Marcos that God forbid they may befall him."

It was "a small, rocky pueblo, all crumpled up." There were seven cities all right—villages, rather—but consisting of no more than five hundred adobe houses. Instead of gold, silver, and turquoise, there was sunbaked mud. Today we know them as the Zuñi villages of New Mexico.

Yet once a myth has taken hold, it is near impossible to dispel.

As they were debating whether to turn back, one Indian, dubbed the "Turk," told them of a far richer land to the east, known as Quivira. Here, he said, "the lord of the land took his afternoon siesta under a large tree from which hung a great number of little golden bells, which lulled him to sleep as they swung in the air" and here even the common people "had their ordinary dishes made of wrought silver, and their jugs and bowls were of gold."

Again they moved on, and after further trials and tribulations, reached Quivira. There was prairie dust, but no gold; the houses were made of straw. (As best can be determined, the present site is near Wichita, Kansas.) Under torture the Turk admitted to lying: he knew of no gold; the Pueblo Indians had paid him to lead them astray, anywhere, so long as it was off their lands. For his belated honesty he was dispatched by one of the cruelest methods available, garroting, and Coronado returned to Mexico, his expedition reduced to no more than 100 men, his personal fortune gone, his health undermined, his reputation ruined.

As was the case with the Cabeza de Vaca party, to the Coronado expedition would go numerous firsts, including the discovery of the Grand Canyon. But this acclaim would come posthumously, not from his fellows but from far-removed historians. His latter years were plagued with ridicule and lawsuits.

It was curious. Then and there the myth should have died. There wasn't even a single golden nugget to support it. But it didn't. The Spaniards had a simple explanation for these failures to find the fabled cities—the flaws were in the searchers, not the legend. When Coronado returned and said there were no golden cities, they accused him of lying. Then they rationalized. Since the plains of Kansas did not contain Quivira, it had to be elsewhere. *Más allá,* farther beyond. In the 1590s the Leyva-Humaña expedition went out in search of it, in 1601 it was Oñate. . . .

Thus was a pattern established. The mines men found were never as rich as those they lost.

If, as Dobie said, modern myth seekers, those who "still have the ability to wonder," are Coronado's children, then the Lost Dutchman, the Jesuit treasure, and a host of other wondrous bonanzas are literal descendants of the Seven Cities of Cibola.

The Jesuits

There *was* gold, however, and silver, and before long the Spanish found it—at first in central Mexico, then later, as the Indian tribes were pushed back, in the northern provinces of Sonora and Chihuahua and on the other side of the Rio Grande.

At first the Indians told them of it voluntarily: it meant little to them personally, except as a malleable metal with which they could fashion pretty ornaments. In appreciation, the Spanish whipped them, bound them in chains, and made them work the mines. Before long, the Indians learned to hold their tongues.

Gold and silver were not the only riches, however. To the men in the black and gray robes the Indians themselves represented another kind of wealth, souls.

One would like to say that the padres treated the Indians better than did the soldiers, but, with few exceptions, they didn't. On the whole, the Indians were not averse to accepting Christianity—western skies were wide and had ample room for many gods—but the priests wanted solitary allegiance. On entering a village they first burned the *kivas*, the places where the Indians worshiped. Sometimes, as in the case of Acoma, they destroyed the whole village, including its inhabitants, as an example to others. As one modern historian has put it, "The Spaniards vowed to turn the Indians into good Christians, even if they had to be killed by the wagon load in the process."

Periodically the Indians would rise up in rebellion against their conquerors. In the great uprising of 1680, even the usually peaceful Pimas participated, burning the missions and haciendas, and filling in and covering all traces of the mines. It was a practice that would be repeated often over the next two centuries and that would play an important part in the history of the Lost Dutchman.

One exception was the Jesuit priest Eusebio Francisco Kino, who arrived in the New World in 1861. Mapmaker, explorer, pathfinder, diplomat, teacher by example rather than force, Kino was, in every way, an exceptional man. It was Kino who first proved that California was not an island; Kino who protested against the involuntary servitude of the Indians—winning from the viceroy their release from the mines and haciendas for five years after their baptisms, unless they were employed voluntarily and paid a fair wage; Kino who participated in cattle roundups, so skilled a horseman that he became known as the "padre on horseback." And it was Kino who first ventured north of Sonora, into hostile Apache territory, to establish Arizona's first missions.

Dozens of scholarly tomes have been written on Kino's ministry. The padre himself left voluminous notes, diaries, letters, and maps. Yet his legendary connection with the Jesuit priests' treasure and the Superstitions is based almost entirely on the *absence* of such written records.

Put most simply, while gold and silver were being discovered in quantity elsewhere in Mexico, during Father Kino's long reign no major mineral discoveries were made in his widespread dominions.

It is part of the legend—for which, again, no written proof exists—that Kino instructed his Indian converts to keep secret the location of such minerals, from all but himself.

If the story is true, Kino's motives may have been entirely altruistic: an awareness that all the good he had done for the Indians could be destroyed by a single gold rush. It can be assumed the viceroy's pledge was good only so long as it was profitable for him to keep his word. Many, however, believe that the Jesuits secretly worked these mines—such as the legendary Tayopa—and extracted vast fortunes from them, hiding their existence from the Crown.

The fact that neither Kino nor his successors mention such discoveries in their writings disturbs no true believer, for the simple reason that the Jesuits were known as "masters of secrecy."

It is at this point that two of the tales meet and blend. According to legend, the Pimas guided Kino as far north as the Superstitions, where they showed him the seven cities of gold. These were the ruins of stone houses of a still older Indian civilization, the Anasazi, or "Ancient Ones." Kino, it is said, realized that the gold, which lay on the houses and ground in such abundance, was the result of volcanic blowout from a nearby mountain, and instructed the Indians to gather it up and return it to the hole whence it came. Only in this way, he is alleged to have said, could the gods of the mountains be placated.

On this trip, some say, Kino placed atop Weaver's Needle the alabaster cross later destroyed by Celeste Jones.

Factually, Kino's connection with the Superstitions is almost as tenuous as his alleged mining activities. But not quite. From Kino's own writings we know that in 1694 he heard rumors, which greatly excited him, of a great stone house and other ruins that lay beyond the Gila River, farther north than he had yet ventured. He made the trip that November, finding, in his own words, "a four-story building, as large as a castle and equal to the largest church in the lands of Sonora." He named the ruins Casa Grande, or Great House, the name it bears today.

Straight across the desert, less than fifty miles to the north of Casa Grande, are the Superstition Mountains.

Kino mentions having made two other trips to this area, but these are not as well chronicled. There is no mention in his works of a mountain range resembling the Superstitions; however, there are two additional pieces of "proof" that indicate he may well have gone this far. One is a map he drew on his return to Mexico, which showed not only the Gila but accurately charted the course of the Salt River just north of the Superstitions (Kino called it the Río Azul). The other is a short account written some years later, in which, describing his first visit to Casa Grande, he said: "On this occasion and on later ones, I have learned and heard, *and at times have seen,* that farther to the east, north and west there are seven or eight more of these large ancient houses and the ruins of whole cities, with many broken metates and jars, charcoal, etc. These certainly must be the Seven Cities mentioned by the holy man Fray Marcos de Niza. . . ."

The Jesuit story is important to the Lost Dutchman for a single reason. The Peraltas later claimed that they first heard of the rich gold mine in the Superstitions from the Jesuits. And Jacob Waltz himself frequently referred to his mine as being on a "church grant."

The Peraltas

Following the expulsion of the Jesuits in 1767, the Franciscans moved into Pima land. Due to the efforts of such militants as the idol-breaking padre Francisco Garcés, the following years saw many martyrs and little mining. In 1827 the Franciscans themselves suffered expulsion. During the next two decades the explorers, trappers, and mountain men—Fremont, Pike, Carson, and Pauline Weaver, for whom Weaver's Needle was named—moved into Arizona, and, right in their footsteps, came the miners, both Mexican and American.

There is no record as to when Mexican miners first invaded the Superstitions, but it is a safe guess that it was in the 1820s or 1830s. Nor is there any record of what they found. But there is a legend.

According to this tale, when the Jesuit priests were finally restored to official grace and returned to Mexico, one of the gray robes was assigned to the town of Arizpe, in the northern province of Sonora. Here, while cleaning the basement of his church, he is said to have found a set of stone maps showing the location of a mine in the lands to the north. Accordingly, he sought the advice of one of his leading parishioners, Don Miguel Peralta, whose family had grown wealthy from the operation of the famed silver mines at Arizpe.

The year was 1847. The Peralta mines were showing unmistakable signs of depletion. Too, a treaty was being discussed (the Treaty of Guadalupe Hidalgo, signed in 1848), which would set up a border between Mexico and the northern territories, bringing an end to Mexican mining in Arizona. Realizing that he would have to act quickly if at all, Don Miguel organized a huge expedition and set out, following directions on the map, arriving in the Superstitions.

On exact details the legend is confusing. According to some accounts they discovered and worked eighteen mines. According to others they dug in eighteen places, following the course of the vein until they finally located the lode in the mountains. (The mining camp of Goldfield, which boomed in the 1890s, was believed to have been one of their mines.)

On one point the accounts all agree: they found gold in almost unbelievable quantities.

Then, sometime in 1848 according to most accounts, on their second or third trip north, there was an incident. It could have been of any sort: the torture of a captive Apache in an attempt to make him reveal the location of additional mines; the rape of a squaw; possibly the defilement of the taboo section of the mountains; or simply the long-standing hatred of the Apaches for Mexicans.

The Apaches needed little provocation. At this time relations between the Anglos and the Indians in New Mexico and Arizona had reached a new low. A bounty had been placed on Apache scalps, and several ghoulish companies had gone into the business of collecting it. A favorite tactic was to invite a whole Apache camp—men, women, and children—to a peace feast, then to feed them meat liberally doused with strychnine. One noted chief, Juan José, was invited to such a feast, then, together with his braves, dispatched with a hidden cannon. Perhaps, since Apache scalps looked like any others, the peaceful Pimas and Maricopas often met the same fate.

As to what happened that day in the Superstitions, accounts are in accord. The Peraltas became aware of sudden danger, abandoned most of their supplies and equipment, and tried to make a run for the open desert and safety. It was only a few miles, through a narrow twisted canyon. But the Apaches were waiting in the rocks above.

The outcome is indicated by the name the area bears today: Massacre Canyon.

Though the exact number killed is disputed, ranging from 68 to 400, it is generally agreed that the whole expedition perished, including Don Miguel Peralta and one or more of his sons.

At least two of his sons, who remained behind in Mexico, survived him. One, Manuel Peralta, was a government official in Mexico City. It was his son-in-law, Ramón Peralta y Gonzales, who later came searching for the family mine and stumbled on the massacre site. And there was another son, named for his father, who in time took over the honorary title "Don," to become Don Miguel Peralta II. He had made at least one trip to the mine and knew its location. It was this son who, some years later, would form a partnership with Jacob Waltz and Jacob Wiser and go to Arizona to work the mine.

The Apaches themselves would later describe—to Jim Bark, W. Irven Lively, and others—what happened after the massacre. While the braves butchered the Peralta mules for a great feast, the squaws were put to work filling in the mines, then covering them over with dirt and rocks so that no trace of them could be found.

It is said that one of these mines was located in a place so difficult of access that the Apaches did not even bother to go to the trouble of hiding it. This mine would in time become the best-known lost mine in the American West—the Lost Dutchman.

There is abundant evidence that Spanish or Mexican miners once worked the Superstitions. Over the years, searchers in these mountains have found Spanish mule shoes, copper teapots, knives, charcoal pits (in which the mine tools were tempered), and *arrastras* (crude smelters in which the Spanish crushed their ore).

The massacre itself is also well documented. In the 1870s Ramón Peralta y Gonzales found sun-bleached skeletons, rotting saddlebags, and gold. In 1913, in the same canyon, two old prospectors known as Silverlock and Malm found over $18,000 worth of loose gold, which they cashed in at the Mormon cooperative at Mesa, before themselves falling victims to the Superstitions. In the late 1920s another old prospector, John Q. Forest, made a careful search of the area and found silver spurs, of the sort used by the Mexican cavalry; flintlock muskets and rifles; cartridges; earthen pots and dishes. Still later, Tex Barkley found a pearl-handled Mexican dagger, among other items.

As for the mine-owning Peraltas themselves, however, evidence was far less definite. As Magill soon discovered, some historians have flatly stated that they never existed.

There was no lack of Peraltas. A Peralta had been a lieutenant with Cortes. Another branch of the family possessed a huge land grant that took in what is today Berkeley, California, while in 1609, one Pedro de Peralta became the first governor of New Mexico and founded Santa Fe as his capital.

One man can be credited with causing most of the confusion—James Addison Reavis. In the 1860s Reavis declared himself Baron of Arizona, laying claim to a large portion of that state and an even vaster portion of New Mexico, by virtue of an ancient Spanish land grant said to have been given to one Don Miguel Peralta in 1748 by Ferdinand VI of Spain. It was a monumental swindle, one of the most ambitious of its time; to perpetrate it Reavis stole countless documents from the archives of Mexico and Spain and forged numerous others, which he put in their place. By the time the fraud was exposed, and Reavis had vanished from the scene, he left behind him a lingering suspicion of anyone and everything connected with the name Peralta.

Still, Magill decided to see if he could track down the legend. With the help of his wife, Melba, who was herself from an old Spanish family, the Valencias, he wrote a letter to Arizpe, addressed to anyone named Peralta. When several weeks passed with no response, he decided to call Arizpe. The international operator, after much searching, informed him that Arizpe, once capital of Sonora, now had no telephones.

Magill knew, from the legend, that part of the Peralta family had supposedly moved to Mexico City. This time his luck was better. After talking to several Peraltas, he finally found one whose ancestors had lived in Arizpe. What was their occupation? He thought they were miners. But he knew little about them and knew of no family records. He did recall, however, that sometime—just when, he wasn't sure—the family had spelled their name not "Peralta" but "Peralto." Magill filed this miscellaneous information in the back of his mind, little dreaming it would ever be important.

For a time he dropped the search. But it continued to bother him. If the Arizpe Peraltas were fictional, then the Dutchman's story of how he learned about the mine from them was fictional also.

Finally he decided to drive to Arizpe. This time there was no excuse that he was going on business. The border officials made clear with their laughter: no one in his right mind would have any reason to go to Arizpe, there was nothing there.

In Nogales he hired a taxi driver named José to accompany him as translator.

Magill had a new car. By the time they reached their destination it was a near-wreck. At Cannanea the road disappeared entirely and they had to navigate the last seventy-five miles via mountain passes and stream beds. It took eight hours, including numerous stops to remove boulders from their path. They arrived in Arizpe in late evening and after some difficulty succeeded in persuading a widow to rent them a room.

It was a short night. They awoke at 5 A.M. to the sound of cannon fire. Its source was the town plaza, the occasion a national holiday celebrating Mexico's independence from France.

After a breakfast of eggs, chili, and bread (there was no

meat, the widow informed them) they decided to attend early Mass, in hopes of meeting the priest. The church was by far the most imposing edifice in Arizpe, a large stone structure built in 1756. Although not Catholic himself, Magill, when at home, sometimes attended Mass with his wife and children. Here he was struck particularly by the odd seating arrangement: women sat in the front rows, children in the middle, men at the back.

Later the priest, Father Flavio Molina, explained that it was a custom dating from the time of Geronimo, when the men sat to the rear to be ready to fight in case of Indian attack. It was here, in Arizpe, that Geronimo's whole family had been killed. In retaliation he had vowed to wipe Arizpe off the face of the earth, and had very nearly succeeded.

Like the rest of the villagers, the priest was openly suspicious of the "gringo." He did take him to the altar, where he pointed to a glass coffin embedded in the floor. Looking down, Magill saw a well-preserved skeleton, clad in remnants of military clothing. He was Captain Juan B. De Anza, the priest informed him, founder of San Francisco, whose body had been recently returned here, to his birthplace.

As for questions about the Peraltas, however, Father Flavio avoided answers, asking Magill to return that afternoon.

For lunch that day the widow served more eggs and chili and, this time, meat. Only later did Magill miss the small dog he had been playing with that morning. He didn't ask for meat again.

Unpacking the back of the car, he discovered several bottles of cold Coke in his ice chest. He opened them and passed them out to the assembled children.

From that moment, Arizpe couldn't do enough for their gringo.

The father of one of the boys offered his services as guide. Magill asked if he might see the local cemetery. If his guide thought the request strange, he didn't show it, but proudly took

Magill to the spot. Arizpe was an old city, with many dead. There were hundreds of crosses, small and large. Since the earth was hard, the bodies had been laid out aboveground, then covered with small piles of rocks. Over the years the rocks had settled, exposing arms, legs, and skulls.

His guide pointed out whole families who had been killed by Geronimo on his raids. Magill looked in vain for gravestones bearing the name Peralta. Oh, there were many Peraltas here, his guide said, pointing to the older section, where the crosses bore no names. Magill couldn't be entirely sure whether his guide, out of desire to oblige, hadn't created the Peraltas just for him. He hoped not.

Returning to the church, Magill found a completely different mood. Father Molina had called in the local doctor to help as interpreter. Though Magill now met the doctor for the first time, he was greeted as an old friend. The doctor had a radio and the only station he received was KOMA, Oklahoma City.

Yes, there were church records, dating all the way back to the 17th century. Father Molina promised to search them for information on the Peraltas, although it would take several days. He would send the information to Oklahoma City. Meantime, while Magill was still here, would he like to meet the Peralta family?

Magill most certainly would.

Only two Peraltas still lived in Arizpe: María Peralta, who was 67, and her unmarried daughter. María, Magill learned on questioning her, was the widow of Emanuel Peralta. Emanuel had been a miner. For some years he had made a meager living working the old Peralta mines at Arizpe. When they failed to produce enough silver to make the effort worthwhile, he had commenced operations to the north, at Muey Prieta.

What about her husband's family? Had she any records relating to them?

No, the family records had been kept by her husband's

brother, who was now deceased. She had no idea who might have the records now.

Did she know anything about her husband's family?

Yes, the grandfather of her husband had been named Don Miguel Peralta. And his father, who was named Don Miguel Peralta also, had been killed in Arizona by the Apaches, along with several of his sons.

They were miners also.*

Later, driving back to Nogales, Magill recalled that in 1849 Geronimo had left the White Mountain Reservation in Arizona to flee to Mexico, killing every Mexican he met en route. What if the date of the Peralta massacre—which had never been clearly established—had been not 1848 but 1849? On his way south Geronimo might well have taken a shortcut from the reservation, which lay just to the west of the Superstitions, perhaps hoping to hide out for a time in his old cave. . . .

It was all conjecture, yet it was just possible that the relationship between the Peraltas and Geronimo was closer than any man would ever know.

Dr. Thorne's Gold

Before Jacob Waltz made his first trip into the Superstitions, another man found gold there, and in all probability it was the same gold that the Peraltas had mined.

In 1865, Dr. Abraham Thorne, a close friend of Kit Carson, was ending his temporary assignment as surgeon at Fort McDowell. While at the Fort, Thorne had frequently befriended the Apaches, at one time curing many of their families of a

* Although for some reason the priest never sent Magill his records, even after Magill wrote to him several times, the information given him by María Peralta was enough to convince him that the Peralta story was true. Historians interested in the Peralta genealogy might well start in Arizpe.

severe form of eye trouble. Late that September, on learning that Thorne intended to return to his home in Lemitar, New Mexico, a group of Apache braves asked him to take a short trip with them, in order that they might reward him for his friendship.

Thorne agreed. That night he was placed on a horse and blindfolded; then, in an obvious attempt to confuse him, someone led his horse back and forth across the Salt River at various points. Thorne mentally kept track of the crossings, determining, when they finally moved on, that they were on the south side of the river.

The following morning, when the party stopped and ordered Thorne to dismount, he estimated that they had traveled no more than 20 miles from the river.

When his blindfold was removed, he found he was in a narrow canyon, deep in the heart of a mountain range. The sun had risen high enough that its rays were just penetrating the shadows on the canyon floor, and looking down at his feet, he saw gleaming dully there a large pile of mineral. Kneeling down and scooping it up in his hands, he found it was almost pure gold, to which only a few particles of rock clung. Amused at his pleasure, the Apaches gave him a sack and told him to fill it, after which he was again placed on his horse and blindfolded.

The blindfold was less secure this time. As they emerged from the canyon, Thorne spotted two landmarks. One was a small quadrangle of rock, which he took to be an ancient ruin. The other was a large peak. Unthinkingly, he commented (one presumes in the vernacular) that it had the shape of the distinctive organ of the stallion. Quickly the Apaches refastened his blindfold, at the same time laughing and telling him that was exactly what they called it.

After leaving Fort McDowell and before returning to New Mexico, Thorne traveled to San Francisco to visit his brother. It was here he cashed in his gold, for which he received $6,000.

In later years, Dr. Thorne made two large-scale attempts to find the place where he had been given the gold. He easily recognized the mountains, which were the Superstitions, and the peak, which was Weaver's Needle, but he failed to locate either the ruin or the exact spot.

As he told one of his companions on the second search, if you drew an imaginary circle, with Weaver's Needle in the center, the place would be somewhere within a five-mile radius. But he never found it, and "Dr. Thorne's Lost Gold Mine" became still another of the missing Superstition treasures.

This name, Magill realized, could be something of a misnomer, since in the various early accounts Thorne never said that he had seen a mine, only a large pile of gold on the ground.

Was this one of the Peralta mines, perhaps the one later to be known as the Dutchman?

Or was it the site of the massacre?

Magill thought the latter more probable, because of two clues. One was the purity of the gold, indicating that it had already been crushed and readied for shipment. The other was that when one emerges from Massacre Canyon, Weaver's Needle does take on one most distinctive shape.

The Dutchman

In his attempt to document the life of Jacob Waltz, Magill drew a number of blanks.

The Immigration and Naturalization Service of the U.S. Department of Justice informed him that the records of all arrivals prior to 1897 were kept in the National Archives. The National Archives informed him that these early records were not indexed, therefore in order to locate a specific individual they would need: (1) the full name used at time of entry; (2) port of embarkation; (3) name of vessel on which arrived; (4) port of debarkation; and (5) date of arrival. If he had all this information, Magill realized, he wouldn't need to make the search in the first place.

He tried a different approach. In his Arizona research he had already found that Waltz had been granted citizenship on July 19, 1861, in Los Angeles, California, in the Court for the First District. In applying for citizenship, Waltz must have given his birthplace, the name of his parents, the date and place of his arrival in the United States, and possibly other relevant information. This time Magill wrote directly to the National Archives, only to find that all such records prior to September, 1906, were retained by the appropriate courts. A letter to the County Clerk of Los Angeles County brought the reply that they were unable to locate these particular records, and had he tried the National Archives?

More frustrating still were his attempts to track down Waltz's ore shipments. According to legend, Waltz and his partner, Jacob Wiser, had shipped more than a quarter of a million dollars' worth of gold to the San Francisco Mint from various points in Arizona Territory, including Phoenix, Florence, Casa Grande, and Pinal.*

For the time and place—or any time or place for that matter—this was a fantastic amount of money, and Magill was inclined to doubt it, believing that had it been true Waltz would have attracted far more attention than was the case.

An even dozen letters were necessary before Magill learned that the appropriate United States Mint ledgers were now stored in the San Francisco Center of the National Archives. An equal number were necessary before permission was obtained for a San Francisco friend to search them.

The search netted nothing. Except for the names of a few individual ore buyers and some large mines such as the Silver

* The most commonly quoted figure is $254,000. Some accounts, however, claim Waltz took out as much as $40,000,000. Had the latter been true, or even half correct, the resultant stampede would have easily dwarfed the California gold rush.

King, shipments were listed mostly under the names of banks, businesses, and stage companies. In Waltz's time, when a man cashed in his gold, the common practice was to sell it to an ore buyer or to a stage line, in this case Wells Fargo.

An inquiry to the History Room of Wells Fargo Bank in San Francisco brought the information that the old stage records no longer existed.

For Waltz's gold, Magill was left dependent on verbal evidence, such as the account, quoted earlier, of the $1,600 sale of two burro loads to ore buyer Charlie Myers of Tucson. There were a half-dozen similar sales—mentioned in early newspaper accounts or recalled by old-timers—to an A. L. Pellegrin, to the Goldman and Company Store in Phoenix, and others. Altogether, they totaled some $20,000.

There was additional hearsay evidence. In November, 1890, Waltz had supposedly given Julia Thomas $1,400 with which to pay the debts of her soda fountain. And there was the $1,200 that Reiney Petrasch dug up from beneath the hearth of the Dutchman's cabin after the flood. But these too were undocumented, although often mentioned in the various accounts. Repetition of these tales did not constitute proof, Magill knew, nor did concensus of opinion.

There was, then, no indisputable proof that the Dutchman had ever cashed in any gold. Why then didn't he give up his search at this point? Magill later asked himself this question. He was never able to come up with a satisfactory answer.

Sims Ely became Magill's primary source for Jacob Waltz's last instructions to Julia Thomas.

An Arizona newspaperman and close friend of Jim Bark, a rancher who had range rights on the Superstitions, Ely had come onto the Dutchman story early and, like Magill, had been fascinated by it. Ely had first interviewed Julia Thomas in 1896, just five years after Jacob Waltz's death. He had talked to her on a number of other occasions, not only checking her stories against each other but cross-examining her on specific details, then comparing her recollections against those of Reiney Petrasch, earlier assembled by Bark. Ely's story had been published in a book titled *The Lost Dutchman Mine*.*

Of all writers on these events, Ely was the most important, both in proximity of time and carefulness of research. Magill had gone over his account so often that he knew it almost word for word. Though he found errors, they were minor and occurred usually when Ely wrote of something of which he lacked personal knowledge. His accuracy was crucial, as most clues to the location of the mine were contained in the Dutchman's last words. A single change in wording ("down the hillside" to "down the mountainside," for example) could send a searcher miles out of his way.

Shortly after finding the book, Magill placed a call to Ely's publisher, William Morrow and Company, hoping to contact the author, only to learn that Ely had died shortly after the book appeared. According to his editor, John C. Willey, now Editor-in-Chief of Morrow, though there had been some editing and revision of the manuscript, care had been taken to keep the Jacob Waltz quotations intact.

Ely's book, together with various city and federal records, censuses, city directories, property deeds, early newspaper accounts, and local lore, finally enabled Magill to reconstruct the Dutchman's story.

Jacob Waltz was born in Prussia in 1810. According to some accounts, he was from a fairly well-to-do family and as a youth attended Heidelberg University, graduating with a degree in

* *The Lost Dutchman Mine,* by Sims Ely, William Morrow and Company, New York, 1953. The author gratefully acknowledges permission of William Morrow and Company to quote from the above volume those portions dealing with the Dutchman's conversations with Julia Thomas.

mining engineering. Other sources say he also served for a time in the Prussian Guard. Though Magill wrote to Germany, attempting to verify both Waltz's schooling and his military service, he found that the records no longer existed.

Nor could he determine just when, or why, Waltz emigrated to the United States. It had to be 1858 or earlier, Magill knew, since Waltz was naturalized as an American citizen in 1861 and there was at that time a three-year-residence requirement. He may have come as early as the California gold rush of 1849; he would have been thirty-nine years old then—but this was pure speculation.

At any rate, he was in Los Angeles in 1861 and moved to Arizona the following year, taking up residence in Yavapai County, near Prescott. At the time of the April, 1864, census, he was living in close proximity, possibly in the same boardinghouse, with two other Germans: Henry Wickenberg, thirty-five, who had been in Arizona for a year and a half, and Peter Backens, thirty-one, who had been there two years, the same length of time as Waltz. Waltz, at fifty-four, was the senior member of this small German colony.*

Local tradition says that about this time Waltz filed a claim by re-emption on the Gross Lode in the Walker Mining District and that for a time he also worked a placer that later became known as the Black Queen claim, but these mining records no longer exist. It can be presumed that Waltz was mining somewhere in the area, either on his own or working for someone else.

---

* The same census also showed three Peraltas in the vicinity: José María, twenty-eight; Concepción, twenty; and Cecilia, twenty-four.
  Neither here, nor in any of the Arizona records, could Magill find a listing for Waltz's partner, the carpenter Jacob Wiser (sometimes spelled Weiser and Wisner). This does not mean that he did not exist, only that he didn't stay in one spot long enough to be around when the infrequent censuses were taken. Then, too, his time in Arizona was tragically brief.

Between 1864 and 1876, Waltz disappeared from sight, at least so far as local records are concerned. These are far from "missing years," however, for it was during this period that he first began to work the mine in the Superstitions.

According to the tale Waltz later told Julia Thomas, he and his partner had drifted down into Mexico, prospecting here and there, when they arrived in the town of Arizpe on a festival day. A gambling game immediately caught their attention. They watched for a few minutes, seeing just enough to convince them they had no business in it. One of the players, a heavy loser, apparently came up with the same notion, for he openly accused the dealer of cheating. There was a sudden flash of steel and the accuser went down with a knife wound in the shoulder. Before the dealer could deliver a second blow, Wiser impetuously clouted him over the head with the butt end of his pistol.

They helped the wounded man to his home and accepted his offer of hospitality. His name was Don Miguel Peralta,* he told them. Over the next several days, as he came to know them better, he told them his story.

Once the Peraltas had been one of the richest families in Sonora: owners of a large hacienda, with many cattle, hundreds of peons, and rich gold and silver mines. But hard times had come upon them. The silver had run out. His father and brothers had been killed by Indians while working their mine to the north. And, for several years Geronimo, Cochise, and their warriors had been laying waste to Arizpe with periodic raids. Now there was almost nothing left except the land.

And the mine.

It was a gold mine, richer than they had ever seen, and he knew its exact location, but it lay deep in the heart of Apache territory. He had intended to return to it someday to recoup his

* This was the grandfather of Emanuel Peralta, whose widow, María, Magill interviewed in Arizpe.

fortunes, but he was afraid of the Indians. However, since they knew the area, maybe they would consider a partnership?

Peralta's offer was attractive. He would finance the expedition—getting together the workers, mules, guns, food, and mining equipment. In return for their participation, he would give them half of whatever was found.

Realizing they had little to lose and that the trip would take them back to Arizona, the men accepted.

They made the trip across the Apache Corridor without seeing a single Indian. Once in the Superstitions, they had no trouble locating the mine, which Don Miguel had visited on a previous occasion. It was everything he had claimed.

"Why, the ore in that mine was so rich you just wouldn't believe it," Waltz said. "The nuggets of gold simply fell out when you crushed the rock with hammers. The mine was a round pit, shaped like a funnel with the large end up. Shelves had been made in the wall as the miners went deeper, and on each shelf stood upright timbers with notches in them for the miners to use in climbing out with the sacks of ore on their backs. The pit was sloping to a point because the workers had shaped it that way.

"Don Miguel's father had started a tunnel in the hillside, down below. It pointed straight toward where the ore would lie, deeper down. But Don Miguel himself didn't do any work on the tunnel, and Wiser and I weren't interested either. . . ."

After working the mine for several weeks, they made their way south to Tucson, where they sold their ore. It brought in $60,000. Peralta gave them half.

At this point, Peralta offered them another deal. Although they had seen no Indians, he was still afraid of Apaches and had no desire to return to the mine. In return for their share—minus a grubstake—he would give them a paper giving them temporary ownership of the mine. The pair readily agreed and, after equipping themselves, returned to the Superstitions.

In describing the return trip to Julia Thomas, Waltz inadvertently dropped a number of important clues to the mine's location:

"Just a few miles from the mine, we found water and we stopped there to make camp. There was water nearer the mine at this time of year, we knew, but it was safer to have our camp some distance away. We planned, actually, to do just as Peralta had done. That is to say, we would ride between the camp and the mine and leave the extra animals hobbled near the camp. Then we'd take each day's cleanup with us when we left the mine and store that gold in a cache near the camp—someplace where nobody could find it. So we got off our horses and hobbled them, and then carefully, on foot, we went toward the mine. As we got near the top of the ridge, we heard noises. Somebody was breaking rock over on the other side. Quietly we crept to the top and looked down. There were two men down there, and they were hammering rock. They were naked from the waist up, and their skins were brown, and with a kind of chill we decided that they were Apaches. . . . We took good aim and we shot them."

But on running down to the bodies, they had a horrible surprise. They were not Apaches but Mexicans, two of Peralta's peons who had been poaching at the mine.

After determining that they were dead, they buried the two Mexicans "down the canyon, where there was dirt we could dig into," and returned to the mine.

After finishing work each day, the pair would take the ore and hide it in one of several caches located not far from their base camp. Over the next several months—the work was much harder now, with only two men—they filled the large cache with about $20,000 worth, and two smaller ones with several thousand dollars each.

Again tragedy struck, this time, according to Waltz, while he had left the mine to go to the Adams mill on the Gila for supplies. When he returned he found Wiser, spread-eagled over the campfire, Apache fashion, like a piece of meat on a spit.

Here the tales differ. There are many who believe that Waltz dispatched his partner and later fabricated the Apache story, which he told on his return to Phoenix. Only Jacob Waltz knew the truth or falsity of the charge, Magill knew, yet an accidental discovery during his research provided a possible explanation for the rumor. In the early 1870s a Dutchman, Jacob Miller, had murdered his nephew while the two were prospecting. Jacob Wiser apparently died in 1871. Over the years Magill could see how first one, then another of the chroniclers seemed to confuse the Dutch Jacobs, until it was Waltz who had killed his nephew, Jacob Wiser. Wiser was not Waltz's nephew, however.

Innocent or not, Waltz felt a lingering guilt for his partner's death. Later he would tell Julia he was sure that Wiser would still be alive had he returned just one day earlier from the mill. According to Mrs. Thomas, the deaths of Wiser and the two Mexicans continued to haunt Waltz until his own death.

There is considerable confusion as to when Waltz actually stopped working the mine. In the Ely-Thomas version, immediately after finding that Apaches had raided the camp Waltz abandoned the mine then and there, staying only long enough to empty one of the caches and to "cover the place over."

For a time he apparently lived in one of the Pima villages, and in several accounts there is mention of a squaw. Eventually he left her and bought a quarter section of land southeast of Phoenix, where he settled down to raising vegetables and chickens.

The purchase of the quarter section occurred about 1875.

According to Mrs. Thomas, Waltz made only one other trip to the mine, to clean out the second of the small caches. "I stayed there only a little while—just long enough to build a rock wall at the mouth of the tunnel that Peralta's father had started. I threw some dirt against the wall to hide the rocks, and then I came away." He left untouched the large cache—which contained about $20,000 worth of ore—intending to come back for it sometime in the future.

Other sources have Waltz working the mine until at least 1884. According to a Phoenix newspaper (the *Saturday Evening Review* of August 24, 1895), "Finally the aged Jacob moved to the vicinity of Phoenix, but he made frequent trips to the Superstition Mountains, each time bringing back with him bountiful supplies of gold. Old Jacob became a recluse and later was seen in Phoenix but once a year, just to vote the Republican ticket on election day. He made his last trip in '84 and brought $500 in two little sacks."

As stated earlier, Waltz appeared in the Great Register for Maricopa County (in which Phoenix is located) in 1876; in the U.S. census for 1880, when he gave his occupation as "farmer"; and in the Register again in 1882 and 1886.

He made the newspapers at least once during this period. Even when he became a farmer, violence apparently followed him. The item, which appeared in the *Arizona Gazette* of June 18, 1884, was tantalizingly short, and there was no follow-up:

> About ten o'clock this morning Pedro Ortega was shot and killed by Selso Grijalva at the home of Jacob Waltz, one mile southeast of this city. The murder was committed with Mr. Waltz's shotgun and resulted from a quarrel over some work. The murderer is still at large.

According to Mrs. Barkley, Waltz was a solitary man, shunned by others because of rumors concerning the death of his partner. In 1888, with the arrival of Julia Thomas* in Phoenix, his life became a little less lonely.

---

* As is true of nearly everyone connected with the Dutchman tale, there is some confusion regarding her name. In the newspapers and city directories she is listed as Julia, Helena, Mrs. Charles, Mrs. E. H., Mrs. E. W., and Mrs. J. E. Thomas.

Julia, "an unusually light-skinned quadroon," has been variously described as "plain" and "incredibly beautiful." On her arrival from Denver, she had a husband, Charles Thomas, but he deserted her soon afterward, apparently by mutual consent. Being a Negro, she was herself something of an outcast, and perhaps this was a bond between her and Waltz. There was said to be still another bond; her mother having been a servant in a German household, Julia spoke Waltz's native tongue. At first their relationship was strictly business; Waltz sold her eggs from his farm.

An advertisement for her establishment appeared in *Meyer's Business Directory* for 1888:

> E. H. THOMAS, Candy Manufacturer, Confectioner, and Dealer in Fresh Fruits, Nuts, Cigars and Tobacco, Ice Cream, Soda Water and Fresh Oysters in their Season. Washington Street, opposite City Hall, Phoenix, Arizona.

In time, the two became close friends. Exactly how close has been much the subject of surmise. Contemporaries of the pair claimed that she was Waltz's mistress. From his experience as a private investigator, Magill knew better than to judge such relationships without supporting evidence. Too, in 1888, Jacob Waltz was seventy-nine.

Close friends they were, however, for in November, 1890, when Mrs. Thomas' business was deeply in debt, due to her practice of extending credit to anyone, Waltz lent her $1,400. The gold, brought to her home, was in tin cans, inside a sack, inside a large wooden box. This, she later told Sims Ely, was her first inkling that Waltz had a mine.

This single statement causes one to wonder, since Waltz's mine was common knowledge in Phoenix. People had been trying to follow him to it for years. That Julia Thomas knew him better than anyone else and still knew nothing of the mine is surprising. With this, and assorted bits of evidence, some writers have conjectured that Mrs. Thomas was all too aware of Waltz's wealth and encouraged his somewhat senile passion for her in order to obtain clues to the mine's location.

The fact that she moved him into her boardinghouse after the Phoenix flood of February, 1891, and cared for him through his pneumonia is taken by some as nothing more than an attempt to extract his secret from him.

Again, it may have been—as the newspapers judged it in Waltz's obituary—simply an act of kindness.

The truth is, no one really knows.

It was while he was recuperating in Mrs. Thomas' home that Waltz first told her and Reiney Petrasch—a German youth who worked for Mrs. Thomas as an errand and delivery boy—of the mine's history. When he became well, Waltz said, he would take them there. They would clean out the remaining cache, the large one, and he would split the gold with them. Because he intended to guide them to the mine, he did not at first try to tell them exactly where it was located, except to say that "The mine and the cache are in those mountains you see over there to the east, the Superstition Mountains," and "The mine is in awful rough country . . . so rough that you can be right at the mine without seeing it."

In bits and pieces he told them of the Peraltas; of his partner, Jacob Wiser, and his death; and of how he had stopped working the mine because of his fear of the Apaches. He also told them of the gold hidden under the hearth of his adobe, which Reiney was sent for. It was, like the gold he had given her to pay her debts, in tin cans, in a sack, in a large wooden box.

Though for a time Waltz seemed to recover from the pneumonia, he had several relapses. It was during one of these, while apparently fearing that he was going to die, that he tried to give them exact instructions as to the mine's location.

"You're not listening," he would yell at Reiney. "You've got to pay attention. That mine is hard to find."

In his final delirium, he dropped a number of clues:

"If you pass the three red hills, you've gone too far.

"There's a great stone face that looks up at my mine.

"From the mouth of my mine I can look down and see people on the old military trail. But they can't see my mine.

"The rays of the setting sun shine in the mouth of my mine and illuminate my gold.

"From my mine I have to climb up to see Weaver's Needle."

One phrase he repeated more often than the others: "I didn't kill my partner. I didn't kill him."

Waltz died on October 25, 1891, and was buried in the City Cemetery, in Block 19, Grave 4, east of the southwest corner of the cemetery.*

Even before Waltz was in his grave, people were lusting after his gold. When Julia and Reiney returned from the funeral, they found that someone had ransacked the house and stolen the box with the gold, which had been hidden under Waltz's bed.

It is not too much to say that Jacob Waltz himself was a victim of the Superstitions, a man whose life was immutably changed by those mountains.

Julia Thomas soon became another. After the Dutchman's death she sold her ice-cream parlor to raise funds for her several searches. She found nothing, but after a time her mind was affected. She married a hay bailer, one Albert Schaffer, and the pair practiced what Phoenix natives called "strange rites," probably voodoo. Schaffer, too, left her, and when she died in 1917, she was living in the worst poverty.

Long before this, however, the search for the Lost Dutchman

* The cemetery has since been moved, and today no one knows where Waltz's body lies.

Mine had begun. Following the lead of Julia Thomas, Jim Bark, Sims Ely, Frank Luke, Frank Kirkland, P. C. Bicknell, and a number of other Phoenix residents organized individual expeditions to find "Dutch Jacob's Mine," as it was then called.

The legend spread.

By 1895 outsiders had heard of it. On August 24th of that year the Phoenix *Saturday Evening Review* told of another search to begin shortly: "Robert McKee, a well-to-do prospector who has been all over the west is in the city to gather data that will enable him to find the mythical mine once known by Dutch Jacob, who in 1891 died in Phoenix."

While the article began by describing the mine as "mythical," it ended "The Dutch Jacob Mine is a reality, and although it may not be found, it is highly probable it will be. One thing certain, the old man took great precaution to conceal the property which must be very rich as he got gold almost single handed."

The article contained one paragraph as important as any other clue the Dutchman divulged. Its source was apparently Julia Thomas. It read: "In a gulch in the Superstition Mountains, the location of which is described by certain landmarks, there is a two-room house in the mouth of a cave on the side of the slope near the gulch. Just across the gulch, about 200 yards, opposite this house in the cave, is a tunnel, well-covered up and concealed in the bushes. Here is the mine, the richest in the world, according to Dutch Jacob. Some distance above the tunnel on the side of the mountain, is a shaft or incline that is not so steep but one can climb down. This, too, is covered carefully. The shaft goes right down in the midst of the rich gold ledge, where it can be picked off in big flakes of almost pure gold."

Apparently McKee was no more successful than the others, as on February 28, 1896, the *Arizona Gazette* reported: "A party of prospectors are now in the Superstition range and the vicinity of Four Peaks, looking for the Dutch Jacob mine."

One story, Magill knew, boded ill for present-day searchers. According to Apache tales collected by Bark, Ely, and Lively, sometime after the Dutchman's death the Apaches returned to the area, not only filling in the pit itself but also destroying the stone face that looked up at the mine, thus obliterating what they knew would be one of its most important landmarks.

CHAPTER 4

Murders, Disappearances, and "Accidental" Deaths

HE COULDN'T put it off any longer. It was a challenge and he was backing away from it. Magill began making plans for packing into the Superstitions. He did so with a full awareness of what had happened to many of his predecessors.

There is no way even to approximate the number of persons who have died in the Superstitions. Some who have gone in and disappeared may well have slipped out quietly, unwilling to admit they failed to find what they were seeking. It is probable that an equal number have gone in secretly and never come out —their names recorded only as missing-person cases elsewhere. Nor is it possible to divide the known dead into simple categories of murders, justifiable homicides, accidental deaths, and suicides. Local coroners' juries seem to have a remarkable fondness for the verdict "accidental death," even when evidence clearly indicates otherwise. The terrain of the Superstitions is the kind where one is not inclined to conduct lengthy investigations.

The rumored toll of the Peralta massacre varies from 68 to over 400. The actual number of men killed by the Dutchman remains in dispute. It was at least two—Waltz himself confessed the shooting of the two Mexican peons to Julia Thomas—and one guess is probably as good as another as to whether, over the years, there were others who came too close to his secret. It is likely that several of the killings popularly assigned to Jacob Waltz, including that of Jacob Wiser, were actually committed by the Apaches.

There are others, fully documented if inadequately explained. In the summer of 1880—when Waltz had temporarily abandoned the mine and settled down to raising chickens in Phoenix—two young soldiers appeared in the town of Pinal and asked whom they should see to get jobs at the Silver King Mine. They were referred to Aaron Mason, manager of the property. Calling on him the next morning, they explained that they had recently finished their enlistments at Fort McDowell and had decided to stay on in Arizona to do a little prospecting. Mason had no job openings but expected some shortly. Before leaving, one of the soldiers asked Mason if he would mind looking at some rocks they had picked up. Several other men were present in Mason's office at the time; as the youth dumped the small sack on the desk, they gathered around for a closer look.

The consensus was unanimous. It was gold, hand-sorted ore, and extremely rich. Where had they found it?

On leaving the fort, they explained, they had decided to take a short cut to Pinal—through the Superstitions. En route they had flushed a deer and followed it up into one of the canyons, where they had lost it. On their way out they had found the remains of an old mine and a tunnel. The rock was from the mine. And there was much more where this came from.

Mason was skeptical. This was not gold in the rough but

hand-picked ore. Whoever left it undoubtedly did so involuntarily, probably during an Apache attack. It seemed unlikely, however, that gold was lying around in quantities described by the youths.

Could they find the mine again?

They were positive they could. It was "in a northerly direction of a sharp peak"—Mason assumed this to be Weaver's Needle—and the country was incredibly rough, but they knew the exact spot. As army scouts, they had learned to observe signs. On their way out they had struck a very old trail that took them over a little gap in the range, not far from the peak, and this trail led them into a valley. The valley, some two miles wide, ran easterly and westerly; following it to the east and after crossing some canyons, they had passed some corrals. From there, there was a trail right into Pinal.

However, they admitted, they knew little about mining; would Mason be willing to go into partnership with them?

Mason briefly considered, then agreed. He bought the ore—even the small sack assayed at over seven hundred dollars—and explained the procedure for posting claim notices. He also helped them outfit for the trip back, and they left Pinal the next day.

They never returned.

After waiting two weeks, Mason sent out a search party. The nude body of one of the boys was found beside a trail leading out of the Superstitions. He had been shot through the head. The next day the body of the second youth was found, killed in similar fashion.

It was an Apache custom to strip clothing from their victims, and the killings might easily have been credited to the Indians, had not another incident occurred at the same time that shifted suspicion.

Shortly after the departure of the boys, a local saloon swamper, ever minus the price of a beer, suddenly quit his job and began spending sizable amounts of gold coin. Mason had paid the soldiers in coin, someone recalled. Interestingly enough, someone else remembered, the swamper had left the same day as the two soldiers and had been gone for several days. Questioned, the swamper claimed to have been in Florence, where he had won the money gambling. A deputy went to Florence to check his story and found it unsupported. But before he returned the swamper disappeared.

Although in later accounts these killings are sometimes attributed to the Dutchman, it was generally agreed at the time that the swamper was the chief suspect.

Mason conducted several searches for the mine, but each resulted in failure. Another man, Joseph Dearing, was more successful, finding apparently the same mine just one year later. One would not go so far as to say he had better luck.

Joe Dearing, a prospector from California, also showed up in Pinal looking for a job at the Silver King. No jobs being immediately available, he obtained work as a part-time bartender in a local saloon operated by Daniel Brown. Dearing and Brown became close friends and Dearing confided to him that after hearing of the death of the two soldiers, he had gone in search of their mine and found it. There was rich gold, he said, only it would take money to get it out. He had decided to work until he could save enough to grubstake himself and a partner.

According to Brown, Dearing told him, "The mine was a kind of pit, shaped like a funnel, the large opening at the top. The pit was partly filled in with debris—Dearing figured it had been washed in by heavy rains—but there was a considerable quantity of rich ore on the surface. He said that on the hillside below the pit there was the portal to a tunnel. It had been walled up with rocks, but one or two had fallen from the top layer, and through that opening Dearing could see that the tunnel pointed toward the pit."

Dearing had also told him, Brown said, that the mine was in

"the most God-awful rough place you could imagine, a ghostly place" and that there was "a trick on the trail—not much of a trick—but you have to go through a hole."

When the job at the Silver King came through, Dearing took it. Here he confided his find to a second man, his shift boss, John Chewing. Chewing, more skeptical than Brown, said he'd believe the tale when he saw some gold. Dearing showed it to him. It was just as rich as he'd said.

Dearing never returned to the mine. A week later he was crushed in a cave-in and died on the operating table.

Elisha M. Reavis was often called "The Madman of the Superstitions." From 1872 to the time of his death in 1896, Reavis resided in a remote part of the Superstition range, raising giant vegetables (a head of Reavis cabbage often weighed ten pounds) and no small amount of local speculation as to why he was never bothered by the Apaches. The secret apparently was that the Apaches thought him mad—it was said he ran naked in the canyons at night, shooting his pistol at the stars—and the Indians held madmen in superstitious awe. Someone—or something—caught up with him, however, for in April, 1896, when a friend realized Reavis was overdue his periodic trip into town, a search was made and his badly decomposed body found next to his campfire. He had apparently been eaten by coyotes, though, from the habits of these creatures, it was surmised this had occurred sometime after his death. His severed head was found some distance away.

Reavis' was the first recorded beheading.

There was no clue as to who killed Reavis. At least one modern writer places his death among the murders the Dutchman committed. Since Reavis died in 1896, five years after Jacob Waltz, this solution seems unlikely. According to older accounts, Reavis and Waltz were friends; they inhabited different sections of the Superstitions and, like the best kind of neighbors, never came visiting.

The same year Reavis died two Easterners—their names were never known—went into the Superstitions looking for Dutch Jacob's mine. Their bodies were never found.

About the turn of the century, two prospectors, one known as Silverlock (apparently his real name was Peterson), the other Malm, began excavating along the northerly apron of the Superstition wall, just where it breaks to the desert. It was not a spot where an experienced prospector would look for gold—nothing about the terrain is right—but over the years quantities of it had been found in the vicinity, along with Spanish relics and the bones of both men and mules, for it was here and in nearby Massacre Canyon that the slaughter of the Peraltas took place. At first their luck was good—they cashed in $18,000 in gold concentrates (not rough ore) at the Mormon cooperative in Mesa. They remained, however, until long after their money was gone, sinking literally dozens of shafts, apparently convinced the gold was native to the region. One day in 1910 Malm appeared at the cooperative, babbling almost incoherently that Silverlock had tried to kill him. Phoenix sheriff Carl Hayden (later United States Senator from Arizona) sent a deputy to bring Silverlock in. He was judged insane and committed to the territorial asylum. Malm was sent to the county poor farm. Both died within two years. Although neither was murdered, both rightly deserve mention among the victims of the Superstitions.

In 1910 the skeleton of a woman was found in a cave high up on Superstition Mountain itself. Several gold nuggets were found near the remains. Although the coroner determined she was not an Indian and adjudged her death of comparatively recent date, no further information regarding her was ever obtained. Nor were the nuggets ever explained.

In 1927 a Jersey City, New Jersey, man and his two sons were hiking in the Superstitions when someone began rolling rocks down on them from the cliffs above, crushing the leg of one of the boys. The following year two deer hunters were driven out of the mountains by huge rocks rolling down on them.

In June, 1931, Adolph Ruth, a U.S. government employee from Washington, D.C., entered the Superstitions with what he said was an old Peralta map. When Tex Barkley went in to look for him several days later, he found his campsite intact, but Ruth missing. That December Ruth's skull was found on the slopes of Black Top Mountain. There were two holes in it. The rest of his skeleton was found in January, three-quarters of a mile away. In his clothing was a cryptic note containing certain directions and ending with Caesar's triumphal words: *Veni, vidi, vici*. There was no trace of the map, however, and setting what would soon become a precedent, law enforcement officials attributed his death to sunstroke or possibly suicide, although Ruth's gun had not been fired.

In 1932 two Phoenix hikers—Calvin Blaine and Ray Schweiger—were shot at by a long-range rifle. Only by hiding behind rocks and waiting until nightfall were they able to leave the area safely.

During this same period, while Barry Storm was conducting his explorations in the Superstitions, he was shot at on a number of occasions. Storm never got a close look at his assailant but he did find his tracks, which indicated the man had unusually small feet. When Storm's book, *Thunder God's Gold*,* was published, this revelation caused a small sensation in Apache Junction, since this single clue pointed the finger of suspicion quite squarely at a local rancher. No charges were ever filed, however.

In December, 1936, Roman C. O'Hal, a thirty-year-old former New York City broker's clerk, died of a fall in the Superstitions. Friends who witnessed the fall said it was an accident.

* *Thunder God's Gold,* by Barry Storm, Southwest Publishing Company, Phoenix, 1946.

In 1937 an old prospector, Guy "Hematite" Frink, came out of the Superstitions with some rich gold samples and a report of being shot at. In November, 1938, Frink was found shot in the stomach alongside a trail in the mountains. A small sack of gold ore was beside him. His death was listed as "accidental."

In June of 1947—sixteen years after the murder of Adolph Ruth—sixty-two-year-old James A. Cravey, a retired photographer, made a much publicized trip into the Superstitions by helicopter in search of the Lost Dutchman Mine. The pilot set him down in La Barge Canyon, within sight of Weaver's Needle. When Cravey failed to hike out as planned, a search was launched, but though his camp was found, Cravey wasn't. The following February his headless skeleton was found in a canyon in the vicinity of Bluff Springs Mountain, a good distance from his camp. It was tied in a blanket and lay on a trail that had been searched previously. His skull was found later, in a hackberry thicket twenty-five to thirty feet from the rest of his skeleton. Despite these extraordinary circumstances, the coroner's jury ruled, "No evidence of foul play."

In February, 1951, Dr. John Burns, a physician from Oregon, parked his car about a mile from Goldfield and hiked into the Superstitions. He was found that night, shot through the guts, less than three-quarters of a mile from his car, near the Peralta massacre site. Although a ballistics expert testified that the absence of powder burns and the angle of the wound ruled out the possibility that the injury was self-inflicted, the coroner's jury brought in a verdict of accidental death.

Joseph H. Kelley, of Dayton, Ohio, commenced his search for the Lost Dutchman early in the spring of 1952. He was never seen again. In May, 1954, a skeleton was found in a canyon in the vicinity of Weaver's Needle which may have been Kelley's. The man had been shot directly from above. His death was listed as accidental shooting.

Two California boys, Charles G. Harshberger and Ross A.

Bley, hiked into the Superstitions the same year as Kelley and nothing further was heard of them. It may be that they slipped out unseen. It is also possible that they had not told their parents of their destination, and their families never knew to contact the Arizona authorities. Three Texas youths, whose names were never known, had vanished similarly a few years earlier.

In February, 1955, four Tucson youths went into the Superstitions on a javelina hunt, armed with .22's. One, Charles Massey, sighted a pig and chased it, leaving the others behind. His body was found the following day, five miles from where he was last seen, wedged between two boulders at the base of a cliff from which he had fallen or been shoved after being shot between the eyes with a heavy-caliber rifle. The coroner's verdict —"Accidental shooting from ricochet bullet." To repeat, Massey's own rifle was a .22.

A month later, Fred B. Stewart, of Chandler, Arizona, collapsed and died on the trail, the cause of his death an apparent heart attack.

In January, 1956, a Brooklyn man reported to police that his brother, Martin Zywotho, had been missing for several weeks and that he was afraid he had gone into the Superstition Mountains in Arizona in search of the Lost Dutchman Mine. In February some javelina hunters found a badly decomposed body near a deserted campsite. There was a bullet hole just above the right temple and a .38-caliber six-shooter with three empty chambers. The body was subsequently identified as Zywotho's, and after tracing the serial numbers on the gun, it was proven that it had been purchased by him. The verdict—"Accidental shooting or possible suicide." Oddly enough, however, the gun was found *under* Zywotho's body.

In April, 1958, a deserted campsite was found a short distance in from the northern entrance of the mountains. There was a bloodstained blanket and hankerchief, a Geiger counter, cooking utensils, a gun-cleaning kit but no gun, and some letters from which the names of the addressees had been torn. No trace of the camp's occupant was ever found.

One Saturday night that December, Roderick White, twenty-six, and his brother Ronald, twenty-two, met a pretty waitress at the Black Swan Restaurant in Phoenix. She was Nettie Isore Maxey, seventeen. When the young men said they were going hiking in the Superstitions the following day, she asked to go along. Once in the mountains the group became separated. After calling her name for several hours they found her, bloody but still breathing, at the base of an eighty-foot cliff from which she had apparently fallen. She was pronounced dead on arrival at Mesa Hospital at 8 P.M.

In April, 1959, two Hawaiians, Stanley Fernández, twenty-two, and Benjamin Ferreira, Jr., twenty-seven, went into the Superstitions, looking for the Dutchman's gold. No one saw them leave. That June a body in a bedroll was found in a shallow grave in a small wash in La Barge Canyon. The body, which had been covered over with iron pyrites, was identified as that of Fernández; he had been shot through the head. Arrested in Honolulu, Ferreira confessed that he had murdered his partner while he was asleep. Fernández had begun acting surly the moment they entered the mountains, Ferreira said. He refused to help dig and "spent all his time practicing fast draw. All the time, fast draw, fast draw." As a final indignity, Ferreira had made what he thought was a rich find, a whole ledge of gleaming yellow metal. Examining it, Fernández, with much ridicule, had pronounced it "fool's gold."

"There's something out in that mountain that drives men mad," Ferreira was quoted as saying by way of defense. Apparently the judge took this into consideration, for, in return for his confession, Ferreira was given a short sentence on the reduced charge of manslaughter.

Of all the deaths in the Superstitions, Fernández' was the only one that ever resulted in a conviction.

In October, 1959, a California man named Steve Hwanawich was found dead in a motel in Apache Junction. In a note found next to his body Hwanawich said he had squandered $60,000 and had hoped to make up his losses by finding the Lost Dutchman. The muzzle of the rifle in his mouth was mute evidence of his failure.

As related earlier, on November 11, 1959, Robert St. Marie, one of the guards from the Celeste Jones camp, was shot to death by Ed Piper on the slopes of Weaver's Needle, while twelve days later Vern Rowlee, of the Piper camp, was shot in the stomach in a scuffle with Ralph Thomas. Both deaths were ruled justifiable self-defense.

On October 23, 1960, a group of hikers found a headless skeleton near the foot of a cliff. The skull, discovered four days later, was pierced by two large-caliber bullets. The body was subsequently identified as that of Franz Harrer, an Austrian exchange student. Although the FBI (called in in this instance because Harrer was an alien) stated that they had a prime suspect, no arrest was ever made. Coroner's verdict—"Death at the hands of person or persons unknown. . . ."

On October 28, 1960—just five days after Harrer's discovery—a skeleton was found in another part of the Superstitions. It was identified as that of a male, in his early thirties, 5'8" tall, with brown hair. A pair of glasses, splattered with yellow paint, led the police to theorize that the man might have been a painter. In November the body was positively identified as that of William Richard Harvey, Jr., a painter from San Francisco. Cause of death was unknown. The bones showed no evidence of foul play.

In January, 1961, a family was picnicking in the Superstitions when one of the children noticed a curious thing: the sand at his feet resembled a human face. Playfully, he kicked the sand away, uncovering a skeleton. It was subsequently identified as that of Hilmer Charles Bohen, a forty-seven-year-old

Salt Lake City prospector. Bohen had been shot through the back. Coroner's verdict—"Shot to death by person or persons unknown."

Two months after the discovery of Bohen's remains, Walter J. Mowry, a fifty-seven-year-old Denver machinist, was found shot to death in Needle Canyon. There was a bullet wound in his head and a gun in his hand, leading to a verdict of suicide.

That June, Davis Galvert, twenty-five, of Phoenix, was hiking in the Superstitions when an "unknown person" shot him in the arm.

That August a sheriff's posse began searching for Jay Clapp, a prospector who had been working in the Superstitions off and on for about fifteen years. Clapp had last been seen on July 1st. The search was finally abandoned.

In 1963 there was a new outbreak of fighting between the Jones and Piper camps. Piper and a companion, Bernard Gerhardt, were accused of robbing one of Celeste Jones' guards of his gun. Charges were finally dropped.

On March 26th of that year Vance Bacon, a thirty-year-old mining engineer from Phoenix, fell 4,500 feet from the top of Weaver's Needle. Bacon and his companion, Ray Gatewood, twenty, of Tempe, had been hired a few days earlier by Celeste Jones to open a mine on the side of the Needle. Mrs. Jones was convinced there was gold in the plug. Bacon was descending on a rope to the spot when he suddenly screamed and fell straight down the east face of the Needle. When his body was finally recovered it was found that his gloves had been burned from his hands by the rope.

Gatewood was left stranded on top of the Needle. While rescue workers—including sheriff's deputies—were trying to reach him by helicopter, two bullets splattered on the rocks near them.

In February, 1964, an elderly New York City couple was found murdered in an automobile parked at the edge of the Superstitions.

In March the camp and headless skeleton of Jay Clapp was finally located, three years after Clapp's disappearance. He was identified by two cameras with the initials "JC" engraved on them. His skull has never been found and the cause of death remains "unknown."

In April two California men searching for the Dutchman quarreled and one shot the other, although not fatally.

In February, 1965, an old campsite was found in the northwest part of the Superstitions, about one mile south and a half-mile east of First Water. There was a set of false teeth, various human bone fragments, and a pillbox with the name Charles Reed, Wenatchee, Washington, and the date 10-3-63. Nothing more was found.

In March, 1965, Glenn D. Magill made his first trip into the Superstitions.

There is a tale, possibly apocryphal, but often told in Apache Junction, that one of the best known of the U.S. Marine Corps generals heard of the Superstitions and decided it would be an excellent area for basic training. With a cadre of officers, the general went to Arizona to investigate. According to the story, they spent five hours hiking in, eleven hours hiking out, and never brought up the subject again.

It was both easier and much rougher than Magill had anticipated. Easier, because there was a clearly defined trail, maintained by the U. S. Forest Service, that led from First Water over the passes through Massacre Canyon all the way to the foot of Weaver's Needle. Rougher, because once you reached the interior and left the trail, it was hell, every step potentially dangerous.

Crandall had warned him of rattlesnakes, scorpions, javelinas, loose rocks, and man. He had neglected to say anything about the cactus. There were easily a dozen varieties, from the giant saguaro to barrels to Mexican ladders, whose spines could spear a man straight through, down to the lowly, sneaky ones that grew in the middle of the brush, jabbing a man as he went by. Magill added tweezers to the growing list of things he should have brought but hadn't.

On this trip he was accompanied by a friend from Oklahoma City who, though skeptical of the Dutchman myth, wasn't averse to getting away from the city for a few days. Once inside the mountains, however, he was less than enthusiastic about Magill's detailed explorations. He rested while Magill set out on his side trips, to see where the Peraltas had died, to find the potholes made at the turn of the century by the ill-fated Silverlock and Malm.

Magill was not lonely. Although he didn't admit it aloud, he had two other even closer companions along. Oddly enough, one was dead, while the other, the last Magill had heard, was prospecting in California.

Again and again in his research Magill had returned to two primary sources: *The Lost Dutchman,* by Sims Ely, and *Thunder God's Gold,* by Barry Storm. Of all authors on the Superstitions, only these two had actually spent considerable time within the mountains, Ely, from the early 1890s to about 1911, riding along with his close friend, cattleman Jim Bark; and Storm, who practically lived here during the 1930s and early 1940s.

Both were convinced by the clues that the mine was located north of Weaver's Needle. All evidence placed both the Peraltas and the Dutchman here. Though each man had conducted extensive explorations in Needle Canyon, Storm had chosen to concentrate his search on one side of it, on Black Top Mountain, while Ely, across canyon, had explored Bluff Springs Mountain. In this way they had almost worked back to back, at least geographically speaking, since a quarter of a century separated them in time.

Magill had studied the photographs, maps, and accounts of

the area so intently and for so long that one by one the landmarks appeared exactly where he had imagined they would be —only larger, far more impressive than any photograph could convey.

Weaver's Needle was like a giant—well—Dr. Thorne had put it best.

Black Top Mountain was just that, dark, volcanic.

Bluff Springs Mountain was wedge-shaped, far higher than he had guessed from seeing it from the air, and surrounded by almost perpendicular cliffs. He was anxious to get to the top, to explore Cañón Fresco, but the sun was already going down—dark came early in the canyons, he discovered—and they still had to set up camp. And it would take at least two days to see all they wanted to see in Needle Canyon and the adjacent area.

Magill slept little that night. He was too keyed up. Also, none of the night sounds were familiar. It wasn't until they were breaking camp the following morning that Magill recognized the site. Only a few yards away was the spot where Adolph Ruth's skull had been found.

During the next two days Magill reconfirmed many of Storm's and Ely's discoveries. He found one of the charcoal beds, described by both, at the north end of Bluff Springs Mountain. On cold nights, the Mexicans dug these, about a foot deep, four feet wide, and six feet long. They would build a quick-burning fire in the hole, rake the charcoal up on to the sides, and cover it with a thin layer of dirt, then climb in and sleep comfortably with but a single blanket.

He found a trail up Black Top, described by Storm.

After a long trek, he found the spring from which Bluff Springs Mountain had gotten its name. As Ely had said, there was an ancient rock dam here, of Spanish-type construction. It was so built, standing about three feet high, as to make a perfect watering place for mules. Yet there was water not two miles away, in La Barge Canyon. If they went to this much trouble, it was for a reason. And there was only one reason that appeared logical, that they were working somewhere in the immediate area. It was from this point, Ely conjectured, that the party had grouped to set out for Mexico.

In a cave nearby, Ely's partner, Jim Bark, had made a momentous discovery: more than a hundred pairs of Mexican sandals, old and of the cheapest kind, with soles of cactus fiber, entirely unsuited to the mountains, but ideal for desert travel. Bark had surmised that their owners had left them here while working the mine and that danger had come upon them so suddenly they were forced to flee without them. This added further confirmation to the tale that the Peraltas had been caught almost unawares by the Apache raid, and again pinpointed the area of their operations; it also indicated that the Peralta party must have been at least a hundred strong.

Magill also found, in Needle Canyon, the spot Storm believed to be the Dutchman's primary camp. Here Storm had found square carpenter's nails and other equipment he believed had belonged to Waltz's partner, Jacob Wiser.

He had not found the large cache, however, and Magill had no more luck.

It gave him an odd feeling, standing here. "From the mouth of my mine I can look down and see people on the old military trail," the Dutchman had said. Needle Canyon was the old military trail. "But they can't see my mine."

Somewhere up there—under a ledge, Magill guessed, for this seemed the only logical explanation—was the Lost Dutchman Mine. There were a thousand spots on both mountains that could fit the description.

If Storm was correct, this was the Dutchman's base camp. He stayed here when not actually working the mine, close enough to see if anyone was in the vicinity of the mine area, yet far enough away to avoid being tracked when he went there.

The trails up Black Top were visible from a dozen different

directions. As for Bluff Springs, it was so steep there appeared to be no way up it.

Yet Magill knew there was a trail, or once had been. In 1911 Jimmy Anderson, one of Bark's cowboys, had told Sims Ely of finding an ancient path up the sheer east side of Bluff Springs Mountain. It was nearly three feet wide and so deeply worn in the solid rock that thousands of mules or other animals must have used it. Ely didn't believe him; in all his searches he had never seen such a trail. But Anderson showed it to him, and also showed him why he had missed it earlier. Landslides or earthquakes had covered over its lower start, while the remaining portion, which began about halfway up the mountain, couldn't be seen from below because of the heavy brush.

Magill feared that further landslides might have completely obliterated it in the years intervening, but after a full day's search that left his clothing in shreds, he found it.

Unfortunately, that same day they reached the end of their provisions. At the outset, Magill had been forced to make a choice between two modes of travel: to pack in with rented mules and horses, which meant a number of people would know where they were going, or to come in secretly, carrying all of their supplies on their backs. He had chosen the latter. And they had had their privacy—from the moment they entered the mountains, they hadn't seen another living person—but it had cost him the chance to explore Bluff Springs Mountain.

It was with a feeling of keen disappointment that he emerged from the mountains at First Water.

Legend had it that whoever came close to the Lost Dutchman Mine suffered a tragic fate.

On this trip he hadn't even found it necessary to take his .38 S/W Police Special out of the holster.

He came back twice that year, both times alone, feeling that the absence of bitching more than compensated for the danger.

The first trip he found the waterholes dried up and had to trek out the second day, dehydrated and exhausted.

The next time, that fall, there was ample water; once he had relocated the old trail, a three-hour climb brought him to the top of Bluff Springs Mountain.

It was a cliché, he knew, but nothing else seemed quite appropriate: as he came over the summit he felt as if he were on top of the world. The view was incredible—the gigantic spire of Weaver's Needle, Geronimo's Head, Black Top, and, thousands of feet below, La Barge Canyon. On the opposite side, he knew, the drop would be just as spectacular, to Needle Canyon.

Bluff Springs Mountain was about four miles long. Its varying width, from a half-mile at the northern end to about two miles at the southern, gave it its wedge shape. The Anderson-Ely trail had brought him up the east or La Barge Canyon side, about midway in the mountain. Once on top he headed straight for the hidden valley spotted from the helicopter. He had no trouble finding it. It nearly bisected the center of the mountain, running for at least a couple of miles to the narrow end of the wedge. Climbing down the steep walls, he found at the bottom no less than five separate pools of clear, fresh water. It well deserved the name Cañón Fresco.

He spent several hours exploring the area. It was a perfect corral. A few men strategically placed at the top could keep all the animals in sight and watch for Apaches. The camp was both hidden and well protected, a natural fortress atop one of the most inaccessible mountains in the whole Superstition range. It was so perfect that he began to doubt it.

Starting back up the wall, but at a different spot, he suddenly stopped. Something dark and metallic was sticking out of the loose dirt at his feet. Even before he reached down and picked it up he knew what it was—an old Spanish mule shoe!

Back on top, he sat down and took several deep breaths, trying to control his excitement. He was unsuccessful. In the beginning he had tried to approach this search as he would any investigation, on an objective basis, by securing the facts and analyzing them as best he could. Now he realized that he was deeply involved.

He had never really thought about it before but he tried to now. At some point—so subtly perhaps that he couldn't pinpoint it—he had stopped doubting and started believing in the existence of the Lost Dutchman Mine.

Perhaps it was when he first talked to Mrs. Barkley and heard her describe the Dutchman. Or when he found María Peralta. Or maybe. . . .

The mule shoe marked another turning point, and with it came a sudden chill, for he was now convinced that if all the clues and evidence were correct, he was at this moment very close to the mine.

In his explorations the next several days Storm and Ely weren't with him. The company was far more numerous.

"There's a kind of trick on the trail—not much of a trick—but you have to go through a hole." The voice was Joe Dearing's.

"It was a very old trail, which took us over a little gap in the range, near the peak." The two soldiers.

"The mine was a round pit, shaped like a funnel, with the large end up. . . ." This was the voice he heard most often.

Oddly enough, his second discovery, made the day after he found the Spanish mule shoe, though more important, excited him less. While scouting the flattop of the mountain, about midway between the two ends, he found several pieces of rose quartz, flecked with gold.

It was not rich, but it was gold, and the Dutchman's gold had been in rose quartz.

But the area where the find occurred fit none of the clues, and a careful search indicated these must be isolated pieces, as he could find no others, nor any outcropping.

By carefully rationing his food, he was able to remain on Bluff Springs Mountain for five days. By the time he went down the voices were mocking him. The hours he had spent trekking over the top, reexploring the hidden valley, and climbing around the narrow ledges over the abrupt precipice on the Needle Canyon side had netted nothing—except an old mule shoe and some pretty rocks that his children would enjoy playing with.

To stumble on the mine accidentally would be a near impossibility.

If anyone ever found it, he would have to have a map.

When he drove back to Oklahoma City it was with the determination to leave the Lost Dutchman far behind him. Already he had spent hundreds of dollars, and wasted even more hours, on this "mythical quest." It would be nice to slide into a big soft bed, his wife beside him, his sleep untormented with hunches and clues.

It had all been a phase—postponed adolescence.

En route back, it came to him. One man had owned a map: Adolph Ruth.

CHAPTER 5

"Veni, Vidi, Vici"— The Death of Adolph Ruth

OF ALL the Superstition deaths, that of Adolph Ruth was in many ways the most tantalizing. It began with one tragic murder and ended with another eighteen years later.

In 1913 General Victoriano Huerta seized control of the government of Mexico, murdered President Francisco I. Madero, and assumed the presidency himself, actions that displeased many persons, including the President of the United States, Woodrow Wilson. Opposition spread rapidly—under the leadership of such men as Villa, Zapata, Carranza, and Obregón—and it became clear that Wilson looked with favor on their plans to depose Huerta. To thwart the new government officially, Wilson withheld recognition and instigated a trade blockade. Unofficially, he made it possible for the opposition to buy arms in the United States.

Raising money for these arms was another problem, as the insurgents were poorly financed and Wilson could not appropriate funds for this purpose. Instead it was arranged that the United States would secretly buy large herds of Mexican cattle, which Venustiano Carranza and his forces would drive to the Texas border, the money realized then being used for guns and ammunition.

A young doctor, Erwin C. Ruth, representing the Bureau of Animal Husbandry, was sent from Washington, D.C., to supervise the border inspection of cattle and other phases of the negotiations.

Erwin Ruth was an unusual man. After graduating from school with high honors and degrees in medicine and surgery, he seemed assured of a profitable practice, when he decided that what he wanted most was to become a veterinarian. Against many arguments, he not only changed his field but also entered the least remunerative branch of his chosen profession, government service, as had his father and brother before him.

In the course of negotiations, Ruth became close friends with one of Carranza's representatives, Pedro Gonzales, former Mexican consul to the United States. On one occasion Dr. Ruth mentioned to Gonzales that his father, Adolph Ruth, indulged two odd hobbies: collecting old maps and hunting for buried treasure. On hearing this, Gonzales gave Dr. Ruth a quizzical look but said nothing.

The scope of operation, as well as the nature of Mexican politics, made it inevitable that word of the cattle deal would eventually reach Huerta. A number of prominent Mexican officials suspected of participation were arrested and charged with treason, among them Gonzales. Through unofficial connections, no small amount of bribery, and consummate effort, Ruth managed to secure Gonzales' release.

In gratitude Gonzales offered Ruth a token of his appreciation. Many years ago his mother's family, the Peraltas, had owned a rich mine in Arizona. They had stopped working it because of the Apaches, but he assumed it still existed, unless of course someone else had found it meanwhile. A map depicting its location and other old and relevant documents had been passed down in the family from one generation to another. Because of his father's interest in such things, Gonzales wanted Dr. Ruth to have them.

Dr. Ruth's own interest in such matters was cursory. However, following Gonzales' instructions, the next time he was in Mexico City he called at the home of Gonzales' cousin, Juan Peralta, and picked up the package, which he mailed to his father in Washington.

This occurred early in 1914. In July the coup came off successfully, Huerta fleeing to Veracruz and Carranza assuming the presidency. Before this happened, however, Gonzales was rearrested and this time no one was able to stay his execution.

It was an incredible story, the sort that abound in treasure tales of the West.

A man saved from execution gives his benefactor an old family heirloom, a map that leads to millions in gold, or silver, or precious gems.

But in this instance, it was, in every detail, true. And it led Adolph Ruth not only to the Superstitions but also to his death.

Apparently it took Adolph Ruth some time to interpret the documents sent him by his son, for it was not until 1931, upon his retirement from government service, that he appeared in Arizona. Over the intervening years, on vacations, he had undertaken numerous other treasure hunts. On one, in California, he had fallen into an abandoned mine shaft, breaking his leg so badly that a silver plate had to be inserted to hold the bones in place.

Adolph Ruth arrived at the Circle-Quarter-U Ranch, on the westerly edge of the Superstitions, early in June. With typical

Arizona hospitality, W. A. "Tex" Barkley and his wife, Gertrude, insisted that Ruth stay in their home.

Ruth made no secret as to why he had driven all the way from Washington, D.C. He was a frank and open man—too frank and too open. There were on the ranch at the time of his arrival the Barkleys, some dozen cowhands, and two prospectors; it wasn't long before all knew that Adolph Ruth claimed to have a Peralta map that he believed would lead him straight to the Lost Dutchman Mine.

Maps to the Lost Dutchman are not uncommon. In fact, there are several Phoenix men who have found their bonanza in the manufacture and sale of such "authentic" maps to gullible greenhorns.* Barkley probably would have offered Ruth the polite attention, and private laughter, accorded any tenderfoot had it not been for Ruth's questions. Although he claimed never to have visited the region previously, he showed an intimate knowledge of the Superstitions, especially the inner reaches where few tourists ventured.

Was there, Ruth asked Barkley, a tall, sharp peak shaped like a sombrero that could be seen as a landmark for some distance both north and south?

There was, Barkley admitted, Weaver's Needle. In fact, the Spanish name for it had been "El Sombrero."

---

* Most common is the so-called "Walker-Wiser" map, sold for whatever the traffic will bear. What is never mentioned is that this is one of the grander hoaxes perpetrated by the late Tom Weedin, an Arizona newspaper editor known for his fine sense of humor.

According to the tale, Jacob Wiser did not die when his partner shot him but stumbled out of the mountains to the ranch of Dr. John D. Walker, where, gasping his last breath, he drew a crude map with directions to the mine.

In investigating the story, several things bothered Magill: one was why the wounded Wiser chose the Walker ranch—since en route from the Superstitions he would have had to pass through three other ranches and a town; another was why Walker never attempted to use the map; and last, but not least, the fact that the Walker family had never heard the tale, until the time Weedin first told it, after Dr. Walker was dead.

Was there a place, within sight of this peak, where two mountains met in a canyon junction?

As far as he knew, Barkley said, only one place fit that exact description—Needle Canyon, between Black Top and Bluff Springs mountains.

What about water? Ruth asked eagerly. Was there a water hole nearby?

There was, Barkley said, but since this was June it was dry, as were nearly all the water holes in the Superstitions, except, of course, for one pool in West Boulder Canyon, which had water year round. But that was miles.

Ruth impatiently interrupted. Would Barkley take him there?

Barkley explained that June was probably the worst month of the year to go into the Superstitions. Water was scarce. The temperature hovered at 110 during the day, and at night, due to the absorbent nature of the rocks, often stayed above 90. Where he wanted to go was incredibly rough. And there were other hazards—rattlers, mountain lions. . . .

Out of politeness, he did not comment on the obvious. Adolph Ruth was sixty-six years old, far from a young man. And he walked with the aid of a cane. Barkley frankly doubted that he could survive the rigors of such a trip.

But Ruth was persistent. Barkley finally agreed to help him pack in and set up camp. But first he must finish transacting some business in Phoenix, and that would take a few days.

Perhaps Barkley thought that Ruth would tire of waiting and abandon the idea. If so, he couldn't have been more wrong. Adolph Ruth had waited seventeen years for this trip. Barkley left for Phoenix on June 12th. The following day Ruth prevailed upon the two prospectors, George Lusk and John Harris,* to take him in, which fact Barkley learned on the 17th, upon his return.

* For reasons which will become obvious, aliases have been used here.

"I had a hunch," Barkley would later cryptically explain—he set out at once for the water hole in West Boulder Canyon. He found Ruth's camp easily, but on examining the dead ashes of the campfire ascertained he could not have been there for at least 24 hours. Barkley made as thorough a search of West Boulder and Needle canyons as daylight would permit, firing a number of rounds and periodically yelling Ruth's name. There was no reply. After contacting the sheriffs of both Pinal and Maricopa counties—the imaginary county line ran directly through the area—he went to First Water, the Circle-Quarter-U line camp where the two prospectors were staying. They stated that they had helped Ruth set up camp, then left him there, promising to return ten days later with fresh supplies.

Barkley formed a search party. The Indians flatly refused to help. If the man was missing, it was because the gods sought revenge for the trespassing of their sacred domain.

The search, unsuccessful, was followed by some half-dozen others that summer and fall, spurred on partly by a reward offered by Mrs. Ruth, partly by the presence of Dr. Erwin Ruth, who had hurried to Arizona at news of his father's disappearance. For the first time in the memory of area pilots, an airplane flew in low over the Superstitions, but nothing but torn country could be seen.

Dr. Ruth finally returned to Washington, heartbroken, and also furious at the Arizona authorities, who had refused to conduct a long search. It was their opinion that since Ruth couldn't last more than three days without water, any further search was unnecessary. They also refused to admit the possibility of foul play.

Tex Barkley was less inhibited. As he told Phoenix newspapermen, he was of the opinion that "Ruth was followed into the mountains and then slain for the map he was known to possess. . . ."

That December a Phoenix newspaper, the *Arizona Republic,*

in cooperation with the Archeological Commission of the City of Phoenix, sent an expedition into the Superstitions to investigate some prehistoric Indian ruins. Things went badly from the start. Music, one of the hounds in the party, stole the beefsteaks intended for supper the first night.

The following day, in disgrace but well-fed, Music slunk along behind the rest of the pack as they proceeded up Needle Canyon. At one point, however, he bounded ahead, up the side of a large mesa, then suddenly stopped in the shadow of a paloverde tree. He didn't howl but stood so still the men thought he had spotted a rattler; arriving at the spot they found it to be something else—a human skull. It was "green," i.e., fresh, with bits of flesh still adhering to it. Picking it up, they observed a small hole in its left side and one much larger in its right.

There were indistinct animal tracks nearby, leading them to believe that a coyote, fox, or one of many other wild creatures had carried it here. A search of the immediate area was attempted but the country was so rough—the terrain broken with gulches, washes, and canyons—that their efforts were hampered. Though they were sure no animal would carry the skull more than 1,000 feet, no trace of the rest of the skeleton was found.

They did find several other things, however. As later reported by *Arizona Republic* staff writer Harvey L. Mott, who was present: "On a nearby hill, an old mine prospect, abandoned years ago, gave evidence of new marks of having been worked within a relatively late period compared to the original working." And: "Some 500 yards south of the knoll we encountered what we took to be a natural hill of some proportions. We were about to circle it following the floor of the canyon, when we noticed potsherds."

The potsherds, or pottery fragments, led to the discovery of the remains of a large prehistoric Indian dwelling. Searching it, they found several smoothly rubbed hand-axes and a number of polished arrowheads. This was on the hill or mound.

"Within sight of the mound, but perhaps 1000 feet higher in the smooth face of a cliff, we saw a great cave which appeared, on examination with field glasses, to have within it a walled dwelling. We were strongly tempted to try to make our way to it, even though from a distance approach seemed to represent an unusually difficult problem." A storm suddenly came up, however, and having placed the skull in a canvas bag, they left the mountains without investigating further.

In Phoenix the skull was examined and compared with photographs of Adolph Ruth. Numerous similarities were noted. It was then sent to Dr. Ales Hrdlicka, renowned anthropologist, at the Smithsonian Institute. After studying photos and dental records Dr. Hrdlicka positively identified the skull as that of Adolph Ruth. He further stated, after examining the two holes, that it appeared a shotgun or high-powered rifle had been fired through the head at almost point-blank range, making the small hole when the bullet entered and the large hole when it exited.

Tex Barkley made another search. On January 8, 1932, he and Maricopa deputy sheriff Jeff Adams made the grizzly find, on a rocky ledge about three-quarters of a mile from the skull's location. Animals had scattered the bones over a wide area, but there was no doubt they were Adolph Ruth's, for the silver surgical plate and Ruth's personal effects were there too. The latter included a medical kit and emergency rations, both untouched; a Thermos bottle, the top of which was off, indicating either that it was empty or that Ruth had been drinking from it when death occurred; his gun, which hadn't been fired; a pickax; his hat and torn clothing; his wallet and checkbook; etc.

Only one thing was missing—the Peralta map.

Ruth's checkbook was in one of his buttoned shirt pockets. Stuffed in back of it, at first overlooked by the searchers, was a single sheet of paper, on which Ruth had written, in ink:

The mine lies within an imaginary circle, whose diameter is not more than 5 miles, and whose center is marked by the Weaver's Needle, which is about 2,500 feet higher, among a confusion of lesser peaks and mountain masses of basaltic rock.

The first gorge on the south side from the west end of the range "they found a monumental trail which lead them northward past Sombrero Butte into a long canyon" quotes from Peralta's map. The monument has been destroyed long. Travel northward, in the gorge and up over a lofty ridge, thence downward past the Needle into a canyon running north, and finally into a tributary canyon, very steep and rocky, and densely wooded with a continuous thicket of scrub oak.

Here the writing ended. Farther down on the page, also in ink but set apart, were the words: *Veni, vidi, vici.*

And toward the bottom of the page, this time in pencil, was scrawled, as if in haste: *about 200 feet across from cave.**

Despite the two holes in the skull, the testimony of Dr. Hrdlicka, the missing map, and the angry insistence of Dr. Erwin Ruth, local authorities declared that inasmuch as there was no evidence of foul play, no inquest would be held. As they told the press, they "believed the aged man's death had been due to sunstroke, thirst, or, perhaps, heart disease." One official went so far as to suggest to Dr. Ruth, who was not content to let the matter rest there, that his father might have committed suicide.

While at least this theory did not ignore the two holes in the skull, it did fail to explain how Ruth had managed to remove

---

* The above wording of Adolph Ruth's last message differs slightly from that given in most accounts of Ruth's death. This, however, is taken directly from the original in possession of Dr. Erwin Ruth.

and bury the empty shell, then reload his gun—all after shooting himself through the head.

I came, I saw, I conquered.

Adolph Ruth's last words haunted Magill, as they had plagued every other searcher for the Lost Dutchman Mine. Had Ruth actually found the mine? Or had the person, or persons, who killed him found it? (Magill had fewer doubts than the Arizona authorities as to Adolph Ruth's fate.)

The story presented a dozen such questions and a host of tantalizing clues.

"The mine lies within an imaginary circle, whose diameter is not more than five miles, and whose center is marked by the Weaver's Needle," wrote Ruth.

These were almost the same words Dr. Thorne had used in describing how the Apaches had taken him to the gold that day in 1865. Was Ruth quoting Thorne?

Magill wrote to the Arizona State Library and Archives, ordering photocopies of all *Arizona Republic* articles dealing with the Ruth search. For days he studied them, attempting to pinpoint the area where Ruth's remains had been discovered, eventually placing it on Black Top Mesa, a spur of the mountain of the same name and a short distance up from Needle Canyon, within sight of Weaver's Needle. This was eight miles by foot from where Ruth had set up camp in West Boulder Canyon. However, Ruth had camped in West Boulder for one reason only, water. All the questions he had asked Barkley indicated his major interest to be in this particular area.

The reference to "a great cave which appeared . . . to have within it a walled dwelling" evoked memories. Magill rummaged through his files and brought out the 1895 clipping from the Phoenix *Saturday Evening Review:* "In a gulch in the Superstition Mountains, the location of which is described by certain landmarks, there is a two-room house in the mouth of a cave on the side of the slope near the gulch. Just across the gulch, about 200 yards, opposite this house in the cave, is a tunnel, well-covered up and concealed in the bushes. . . ." Above this tunnel was the mine, "the richest in the world, according to Dutch Jacob."

Had Ruth seen the article and been looking for the house in the cave and the tunnel?

"About 200 yards, opposite this house in the cave . . ."; this was from the 1895 article.

"About 200 feet across from the cave" were probably the last words Adolph Ruth had ever written.

Something else about the Ruth story bothered Magill, but, try as he might, he couldn't put his finger on it.

One night, in mid-December, he woke from an unsound sleep and knew what it was. It was a small thing, but something that seemed wrong, out of character.

If Ruth, he reasoned, was a collector of old maps, a man who appreciated both their rarity and their historical value, then it would seem highly unlikely that, knowing the difficulty of the terrain, he would carry the original of that precious document into the mountains with him. It seemed far more probable that he would carry a photograph or a copy.

In the lore of the Dutchman, the Ruth story closed with the discovery of his body. It was presumed there was only a single copy of the map. In his business Magill had learned to weigh presumptions carefully before accepting them.

If the original copy of the map still existed, quite possibly it was still in the possession of some member of Adolph Ruth's family. Ruth had two sons, Earl A., the elder, and Erwin C. It could be that both were dead, but they might have children still living. These could be living anywhere, however, and to locate them would necessitate a major missing-person investigation.

Magill started with what he had—the last known residence

of the Ruths. Going to the Oklahoma City telephone office, he obtained the Washington, D.C., directory and looked up the name "Ruth." There may have been ten listed, or fifty—Magill never knew, for he immediately spotted one name: *Ruth, Erwin C., Dr.*

Magill tried to suppress his excitement. It was just a hunch, he reminded himself, and quite possibly just another of the many blind leads he had followed since embarking on his search.

Realizing how important it could be, he spent several days considering his next step, when what he really wanted to do was catch the next plane to Washington, D.C. If he approached Ruth at the wrong time, or in the wrong mood, his cooperation might end right there. In any event, a personal visit would have to be preceded by a telephone call. It was mid-December, a hectic time for anyone. Impatiently—for despite his attempts to play down his excitement, he felt, instinctively, that he might be onto something—he waited until after Christmas. Early on the evening of December 26—Ruth would probably just have finished dinner, he reasoned, and be in a relaxed frame of mind—he placed the call.

Ruth himself answered.

Magill identified himself, explaining that for some years he had been attempting to track down the true story of the Lost Dutchman Mine. He further explained how he had attempted to approach this on a scientific basis and how, like Ruth's father, he had come to believe that the mine really existed.

Magill did his best possible job to sell himself.

And, for a long moment, as Dr. Ruth remained silent, he was sure he had failed.

"Young man," he finally said, "I suppose you realize you've awakened many painful memories for me, things I've tried not to think about for many years. . . ."

How stupid of him not to have realized it earlier! The tone

was unmistakable. Dr. Ruth had given his father the maps. He was still carrying a heavy burden of guilt for his father's death.

"But you sound sincere. I'll tell you what I can. Just what is it you want to know?"

Magill said that he was interested in the Peralta map obtained from Gonzales.

"Maps," Dr. Ruth corrected him. "There were three of them —although for some reason all the writers on my father have fastened onto the idea that there was only one. But there were three."

Magill tried to weigh this new information. But he was unable to suppress the disappointment occasioned by Dr. Ruth's use of the past tense.

He explained, though less confidently, that from what he had read of Dr. Ruth's father, it did not seem logical that he would carry the original maps into the mountains with him.

"No," Dr. Ruth replied, "my father took the originals with him"—Magill's heart sank—"but he did leave a set of tracings." When Ely and the others had called on him, Ruth continued, they hadn't asked about them, and he hadn't mentioned them. He was not quite sure why. Part of the reason, he supposed, was that he did not want to feel responsible for sending any man to his death.

"It's odd," he said thoughtfully, "I'm not sure exactly why I chose to mention them to you now. I've never even met you, but you seem sincere about this. Perhaps it's because I'm in my seventies—even older than my father when he died—and I've always hoped that sometime, before I die, someone will find the answer to what happened."

This was sufficient encouragement. Magill asked the question before Ruth had second thoughts.

"Yes," he replied just as quickly, "I'll send you copies." However, he was very busy, he explained. Although retired from practice, he was on the boards of several funds and foundations, also active as secretary of the Lincoln Continental Owners' Club. He didn't know when he could find time to have them photographed. In fact, he didn't know exactly where, in his mass of papers, the maps were. He had no secretary and would have to look for them himself. He was sure he still had them, however. At least he was sure he hadn't thrown them out. But after thirty-five years. . . .

Too, he didn't know how much help the maps would be. For there was a secret to interpreting them, one that had taken his father years to solve. And he didn't know what it was.

Magill habitually picked up the mail at the post office early each morning, after taking his children to school. He now stepped up his visits to twice daily, then three times, synchronizing them with the arrival times of out-of-state mail.

Every possible fear ran through his mind. That the maps might have been thrown out accidentally. That Ruth, on reconsidering the brash, presumptuous call, might have changed his mind. He had written Ruth three days after the call, thanking him for his courtesy and telling him how much he was anticipating the arrival of the maps—then worried for several days that the letter might have offended Ruth. He could not risk a second call.

The maps had become an obsession. 1965 merged into 1966, with still no word. Even on New Year's Day, when there was no mail, he went to the post office anyhow, just to make sure.

On the morning of Wednesday, January 5, 1966, when he looked through the window of his box, he saw a large brown envelope postmarked Washington, D.C. In his eagerness to open it, he nearly destroyed the contents.

CHAPTER 6

The Secret of the Maps

THE LETTER from Dr. Ruth began with an apology. So far he had been able to find only one of the maps, though he believed it was the one his father considered most important. As for the others, he was sure they were around somewhere, and he promised to forward them as soon as he had time to make a thorough search.

Ruth had not sent him a photograph. The paper was brittle, the ink faint in spots. It appeared to be the original tracing.

Later Magill would try to remember driving home from the post office. He couldn't. He could recall only that he had kept one hand on the wheel, holding the map open with the other. If he had looked at the street ahead, he did not remember seeing it.

Some of the clues were easily decipherable. Although Magill knew only oral Spanish, his wife, Melba, read the language well; so with the aid of Spanish dictionaries, they quickly succeeded in translating most of the words.

(*To follow the clues, see Map A.*)

On the left side of the map was a sharp peak, identified as El Sombrero. This was Weaver's Needle. Traveling around the Needle, as Magill had done both by air and on foot, the mountain took on a different shape for almost every degree of the compass. From various spots it looked like a heart, the hat from which came its Spanish name, and as Dr. Thorne had observed, "the distinctive organ of a stallion." Yet, although there was something vaguely familiar about the way it was depicted here, Magill could not recall having seen it assume this exact configuration.

On the right side of the map was another tall peak, labeled S. Sima, or "South Peak," the old Spanish designation for the mountain now called Miner's Needle.

Magill thus knew two of the major landmarks.

Immediately in front of Weaver's Needle was a third but unidentified mountain, toward the middle of which was depicted a Caverna con Casa, or "Cave with House." Ruth *had* been looking for this landmark. And, from the *Arizona Republic* article, Magill thought he knew where it was located: on Black Top Mesa, a short distance from Black Top Mountain, up Needle Canyon.

There was only one trouble. The mountain depicted here just didn't look like Black Top.

Jutting out from behind Miner's Needle was a fourth mountain. Between it and the third mountain was a canyon or draw. This was the junction Ruth had asked Barkley about; Barkley had identified the spot as Needle Canyon. But Magill knew this area well, and it didn't fit the drawing on the map.

In the canyon was a spot marked *Agua,* which of course meant "water." This could be important, since there was a limited number of water holes in the Superstitions. There was

Bluff Springs, one in West Boulder Canyon, another in La Barge Canyon, the one in Needle Canyon itself, and a few others. Yet were the water holes in Peralta times the same as those today? The years could have brought about a hundred metamorphoses. The Superstitions had known at least one major earthquake during the last century.

The paradoxical fourth mountain interested him most. Everything about it was almost familiar—but not quite.

Toward the base of this mountain, or a small distance up the side, was the word *túnel*. Below my mine the Peraltas had started a tunnel, the Dutchman said. On leaving the mine for the last time, he had placed some rocks across the entrance. There was a tunnel below the mine, Joe Dearing said. He had knocked down the rocks to look in.

Slightly higher on the map was the word *escardadia*. Magill checked his small Spanish dictionary; it wasn't listed. Nor could he find it in the larger dictionaries at the Oklahoma City library. He consulted his wife. She knew of no such word but wondered if it might be another, misspelled. Education was a rarity in the time of the Peraltas. The closest to it was *escardadera*, a "garden implement" or "weed hook." Did this make sense? Magill thought not. Several other possibilities came to mind: *escondido* "hidden, concealed"; *escarpada* "steep, rugged, craggy"; *escarpadura* "scarp, escarpment, cliff, bluff." Any one of these could fit the terrain depicted.

Magill moved on to the next clue, an odd-shaped mass farther up the slope of the mountain. This could be the top of another mountain or hill in the background. Or it could be the "stone face" the Dutchman had referred to, the one that looked up to his mine, the key landmark the Indians had destroyed. Magill recalled Ruth's last message, which mentioned a monumental trail on which the monument had been destroyed.

Above this was the most important word of all—*hoya,* or

"pit," in search of which Adolph Ruth and at least two dozen others had given their lives.

For the first time Magill was struck with a sense of enormity. If he could identify this mountain and locate this pit, he would have found the Lost Dutchman Mine!

In his mind there was no doubt that the Peralta's pit and the Dutchman's mine were one and the same. Too much evidence linked them for him to believe otherwise.

The map was in two sections. The top portion, on which the above clues were shown, was a *perfil mapa,* or "profile map." The bottom half bore the words *mapa del desierto,* or "map of the desert," and the trail depicted was, he guessed, probably the route followed by the Peraltas from Sonora through the desert to the Superstitions.

On the left side, starting about halfway down, were the "keys," five in number. Reading downward, these were a feathered arrow, the figures "15,000," the letter *D,* a snake, and the legend "E to W to N to S."

Barry Storm had included a list of Spanish and Indian treasure symbols in his book *Thunder God's Gold,* as had J. Frank Dobie in *Coronado's Children.*

An arrow slanting upward ⟶ indicated either the trail to a treasure or other signs farther on.

Two crossed arrows ⨯ meant the treasure was divided, and pointed to the different parts.

A downward pointing arrow ⟶ meant the treasure was here, at this spot.

However, the map's arrow was feathered ⟫⟫⟶ , giving it another, or one of several possible meanings: Travel opposite direction. Reverse directions. Turnabout.

There was an *N* at the top of the map. Magill had automatically assumed this meant north. Did the arrow mean this was in reality south? Or did it mean that at a certain point along the trail one reversed directions? There would appear to be any number of possibilities.

What did the "15,000" mean? If a measurement, 15,000 what? Certainly not feet or yards, as the Spanish used their own measurements. Magill called a Spanish scholar at the University of Oklahoma, who told him that the basic unit of measurement in Spanish-speaking countries was the *vara*. This was not a set measure but varied, depending on the country, from approximately 32 to 42 inches. "What about Mexico?" Magill asked. "32.99 inches," the man replied. Changed to feet, 15,000 *varas* would be roughly 41,237 feet, or nearly eight miles. Obviously, since there was no mountain so large, this wasn't the distance between the tunnel and the pit, or even between the Caverna con Casa and the tunnel. Was, then, another form of measurement being used? Or might it indicate some kind of triangulation? Magill didn't know.

The *D* was not listed as a treasure symbol. Spanish dictionaries gave it as an abbreviation for "Don." Was this in effect the same as a signature—meaning the map was drawn by Don Miguel Peralta? Or was it something else entirely? Again, far back in his mind, Magill recalled something familiar—but the more he tried to capture it, the farther it moved.

When a snake traveled downward ⸠, it meant treasure on this side. When it traveled in a straight or horizontal line ∽, it pointed to the treasure. This snake was traveling upward ⸡, which meant treasure on the opposite side.

This seemed clear: the pit was located on the opposite side of the map.

But it was so obvious that Magill began to distrust it. It was not uncommon for a clue to have more than one meaning. If true in this case, what could its other meaning or meanings be?

In his mind, in that realm of the almost recognizable, for some reason the *D* and the snake seemed to go together.

The final clue was the legend "E to W to N to S." Were these directions? So many steps east, then so many west, and so on? If so, how far in each direction? 15,000 steps? Or did they mean something else?

The easiest way to "solve" the map, Magill knew, would be to place himself in the spot where the artist stood when he drew it.

In his trips over and into the Superstitions, he had taken more than three hundred snapshots. Most of these were in color and had been converted into slides. Darkening his office, he viewed them, one by one, against the wall, trying to determine whether any matched the terrain depicted. None did.

Next he sorted through them, trying to place them roughly in the order in which the scenes naturally appeared. He would then mentally project himself a few degrees to the left or to the right, trying to see if a slight change in position made the difference. It didn't.

He studied photos of each individual mountain to see if its contours matched either of the unidentified mountains on the map. None matched. He studied paired mountains that formed canyons, draws, and arroyos. Without success.

He then tried a new tack, starting at the south or bottom of the map and following the route from Mexico. This took him up off the desert floor, across the King's Ranch and the foothills, over the palisades, into the interior of the mountains, and up behind the south side of Weaver's Needle, facing north.

None of the evidence discovered by Ely, Storm, or Magill himself had been on the south side of the Needle. Everything— including Waltz's final instructions, the area of Adolph Ruth's interest, the Spanish mule shoe, and other artifacts—placed the mine somewhere north of the Needle.

This could be why no one had found it to date.

Yet Magill had a photograph of the Needle from this exact

area, the south side, and it bore no resemblance to the shape of the mountain on the map.

The more he pondered it, the more the feathered arrow seemed to be the key to the whole thing. And the enigma.

If he took it literally and, on arriving at the south side of the Needle, turned about or reversed his direction, it would take him right back to Mexico over the same route.

Was it possible that the snake meant not that the treasure was on the opposite side of the map but that it was on the opposite side of the Needle?

Locking the map in the filing cabinet, he went to bed with a severe headache. Each thing could be just as it appeared, or it could be its opposite. North could be south, or maybe even east or west. He felt turned inside out. And in his dreams the map continued to haunt him, only now it appeared as the negative of a photograph, where black became white and white black.

For the next several weeks he spent every free minute studying the map—conjecturing, trying different angles, stopping and beginning again until gradually his disappointment reached the point where he couldn't think of the piece of paper without grimacing.

Adolph Ruth had obtained the map in 1914, but not until 1931 had he begun his search. If it had taken Ruth—who had experience with treasure maps—seventeen years to unravel the map's secret, he might spend as much time and not get it even then.

The horrible thing—that which gave him nightmares—was the damned familiarity of this scene, as if he had seen it often, yet with everything just opposite to where it should be.

Every time he locked the cabinet he vowed it would stay locked. And sometimes he'd keep the vow for a few days. But then he would find himself again darkening the room and going through the tray of slides. One night in late February he found himself there, eyes smarting, and couldn't even remember coming into the room and turning on the projector. Resignedly, he decided to turn off the machine, box it up, and consign it to the closet.

Automatically he ran through the last slides in the tray. Then he spotted it.

It was a shot taken from the helicopter, from high above Needle Canyon, just a few seconds before he first saw the hidden valley. From above, the winding canyon took on the exact form of the snake!

Just past the head of the snake, the canyon branched off, then back, forming a perfect D! (*See photo #5.*)

He'd seen this particular slide a hundred times, but each time his mind had skipped on to the hidden valley on Bluff Springs.

Assuming then, just for conjecture, that this was Needle Canyon, these two mountains would have to be Black Top and Bluff Springs.

He took out the map, at the same time flashing a scene of Needle Canyon as it appeared, with the mountains on either side.

There was no resemblance.

He snapped off the projector. He couldn't hear the voices—but he felt them. He had the distinct feeling that the Peraltas were laughing at him.

Having failed to decipher the first map, he now placed his hope in the two other maps Dr. Ruth had mentioned but, as yet, failed to send. He wrote a letter and, when this brought no response, finally called Washington. No, he hadn't found them, Dr. Ruth explained, because he just hadn't had time to look for them.

Although Ruth was unfailingly polite, Magill sensed his displeasure at these periodic invasions of privacy. All one could do was wait, impatiently.

They arrived the last week in March.

These were tracings made by Dr. Ruth himself.

The second map (*see Map B*) was apparently a more detailed charting of the route from Sonora.

Looking at the third map (*see Map C*), Magill knew it to be the locator map, pinpointing the exact location of the mine. Like the first map, it was divided into two parts. Printed across the center, separating the two halves, was the legend: JUNE 1860 PERALTO. This confirmed the information given to him in telephone calls to Mexico City—the family name had been spelled two ways.

The bottom half corresponded to the top half of the first map, only it showed the canyon junction from an overview.

In the top half, Weaver's Needle assumed the same puzzling shape as on Map A. There was also a series of marks resembling stairsteps, whose meaning eluded him, and several familiar signs: X indicating the mine and /=/=⊂ depicting a tunnel.

The marks were unconnected, however. Might this mean, as the Dutchman had said, that while the Peraltas had started the tunnel, hoping to intersect the vein from below, they had failed to hit it and had left it unfinished?

Having the locator map was no help, not if he didn't know on which mountain the tunnel and mine were located.

For more than a week he studied the new maps, finally having to admit that although he now possessed all three of the maps Adolph Ruth had carried with him to his death, he still hadn't found the answer.

It was an evening in mid-April. Having deposited the family at Silver Lake, an Oklahoma City amusement park just opened for the season, he was alone in his study.

Again he returned to the first map and the feathered arrow. Travel opposite direction. Reverse directions. Turnabout.

What if—a sudden chill moved up his spine—*what if this actually meant reverse everything—put the mountain that's on the left on the right, and the mountain on the right—*

Mentally, he tried it, then realized there was a much easier way. Running to a mirror, he held up the map in front of it. Suddenly everything was in its proper place. There was no need to turn on the projector to visualize the scene. He was standing in the vicinity of the Three Red Hills, looking up Needle Canyon, with Black Top Mesa on his right and Bluff Springs Mountain on his left. And for the first time Weaver's Needle assumed its familiar shape.

The pit—the Peralta mine—the Lost Dutchman Mine—*was* north of the Needle. On the rugged cliffs of Bluff Springs Mountain!

He had been wrong in assuming the bottom half of the first map was the map of the desert. Now it was reversed, he could see it was the route the Peraltas would have followed up La Barge Canyon to the Needle Canyon junction, while the words at the bottom, *mapa del desierto,* apparently meant that the second map took up where the first left off. This could explain the "15,000" figure; it could be *varas* after all. It was about eight miles from the edge of the Superstitions to the Needle Canyon junction over this route.

Lest the map fall into the wrong hands, the Peraltas had devised a simple, but quite effective, trick. They had reversed it. By holding it up to a mirror or—better yet—to sun or other light and looking through it from the opposite side, everything was transposed.

Hurriedly he got out the other two maps and held them up to the mirror. For a moment a puzzled frown appeared on his face, which suddenly gave way to a wide grin. He had underrated the Peraltas. The trick was more complex than he had first thought. They had only reversed some of the maps.

The first map had been reversed, as had the third. The key

was the reversed figure of Weaver's Needle, which appeared on both. But the second map, which showed the Peralta's route from Mexico, hadn't been changed.

In studying the bottom half of the third map correctly for the first time he noticed something missed earlier. The two canyons that met in a junction were La Barge and Needle. And the mountain on which the large X and the word *Mine* appeared? It was Bluff Springs.

Thus his discovery was confirmed two ways!

Adolph Ruth must have experienced this same feeling, Magill realized, when he finally discovered the secret.

The snake did have two meanings. It was Needle Canyon. And it was also a private joke. For in turning over the map the treasure was indeed on the opposite side.

He had actually located the Lost Dutchman Mine! Magill felt no doubt of it. And yet, in the midst of his excitement, he also sensed another emotion, something he couldn't define, almost a feeling of regret, or loss. He had lived with this thing so long.

A conversation between Ed Piper and Robert Crandall, related to him by Crandall on his last trip to Albuquerque, came to mind. One night, shortly after Celeste Jones and her crew had packed up and left the Superstitions, and not long before Piper's own death, the two men had been sitting around their campfire on the slope of the Needle. All was quiet. They had been talking of the Jesuit treasure but their words were applicable to the Lost Dutchman as well.

Crandall had said, "Did you ever think, Ed, what we would do if we actually found the treasure?"

A pained, stricken look passed over Piper's face. "What would we do, Bob? Where would we go from there?"

MAP A

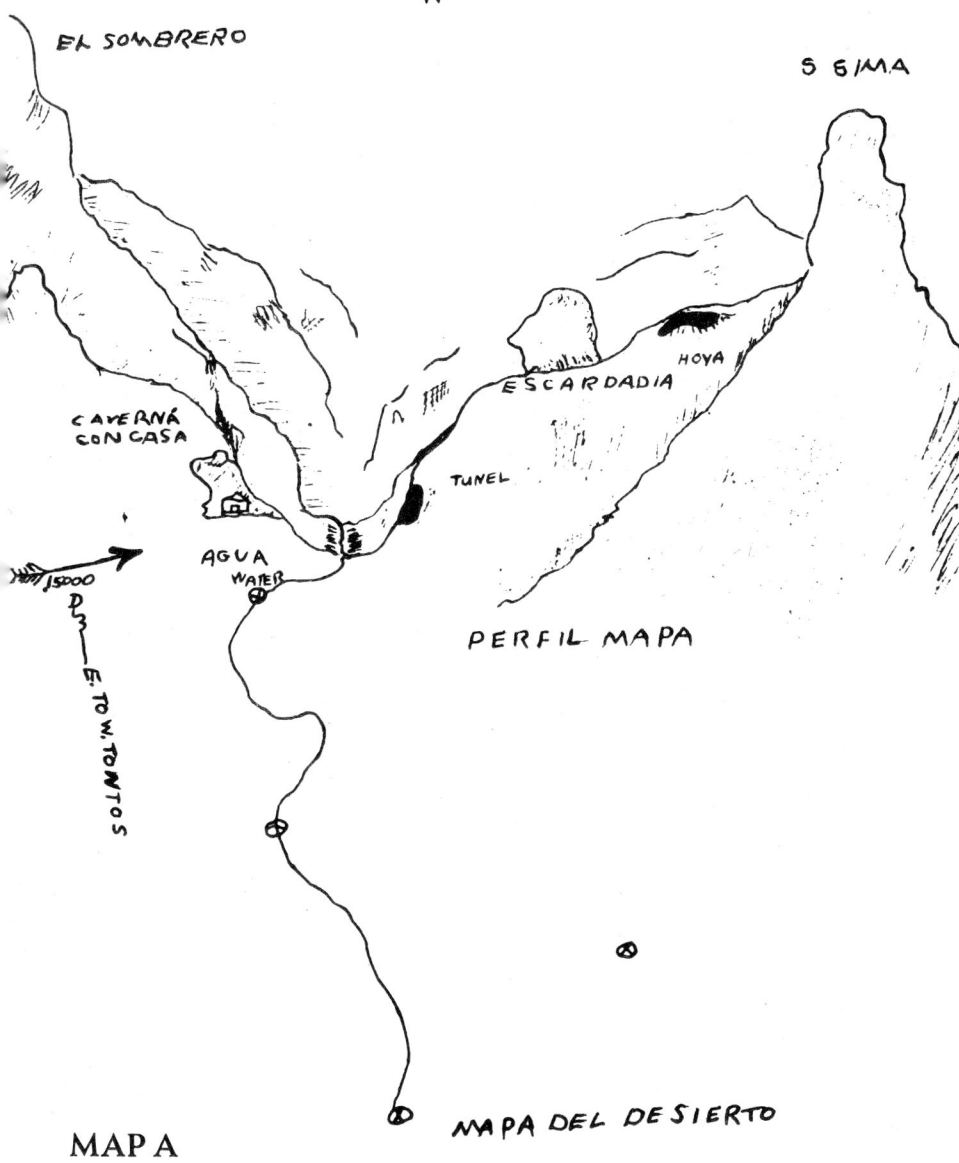

The first Peralta-Ruth map. To keep treasure hunters from
finding the mine, the Peraltas used a trick: they reversed the map.
To put the landmarks in their correct place, hold the map
before a mirror. The keys and symbols are explained in the text.
(Courtesy Erwin Ruth and Glenn Magill)

To see how the landmarks fit, compare this photo of Needle Canyon with the reversed Map A. On the left is Bluff Springs Mountain, site of the Lost Dutchman Mine; on the right, Black Top Mountain; and, in the background, Weaver's Needle. Miner's Needle, shown on the map as S. Sima, does not appear in this particular photo. *(Courtesy Glenn Magill)*

MAP B

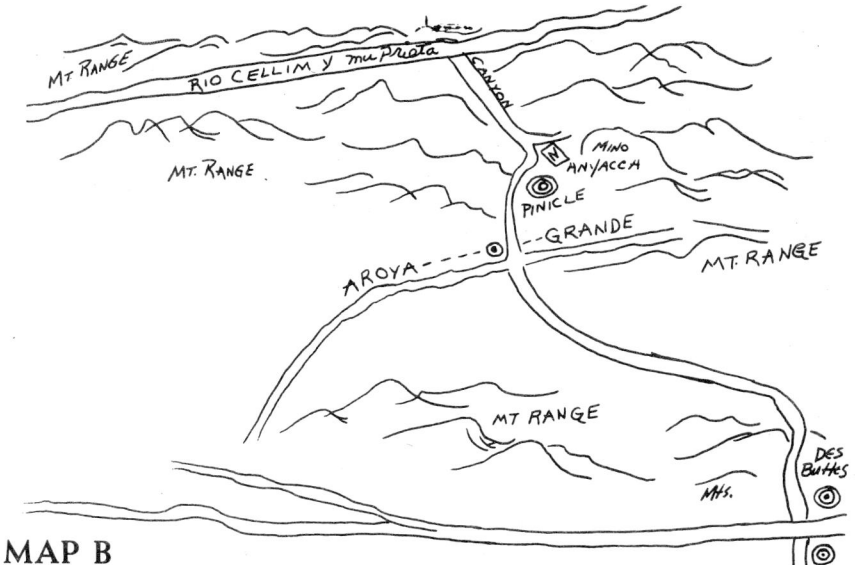

This map, which is not reversed, shows the route the Peraltas followed from Mexico into the Superstition Mountains of Arizona. The landmarks are identified in the text. *(Courtesy Erwin Ruth and Glenn Magill)*

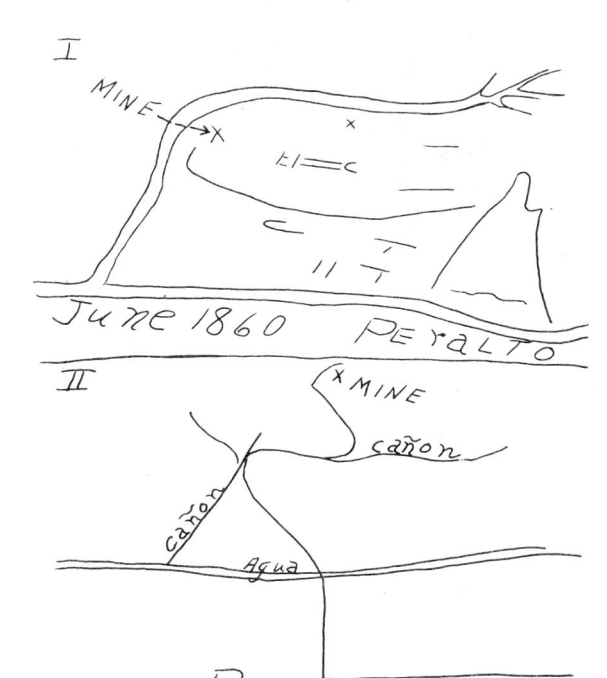

MAP C

Also reversed, this is the locator map, which shows exactly where the mine is located. The keys and symbols are interpreted in the text. *(Courtesy Erwin Ruth and Glenn Magill)*

Andy Vloedman breaking Satan, preparatory to the discovery trip. The incident aroused some unappreciated humor.
(Courtesy Glenn Magill)

Word reached Apache Junction that a small army had invaded the Superstitions. Left to right, Andy Vloedman, Carl Lee, Satan, Pauline, and Baker Looney. *(Courtesy Glenn Magill)*

Bluff Springs Mountain. All clues placed the Lost Dutchman Mine on these rugged cliffs on the westerly side. The first arrow from the right points to the tunnel area, the second to the pit above it, the third to the area of the "vanishing pit."
(Courtesy Glenn Magill)

Needle Canyon, as seen from the tunnel area on Bluff Springs Mountain. Note how the canyon forms a "D" and a "snake."
(Courtesy Glenn Magill)

Glenn Magill on guard duty atop Bluff Springs Mountain. This was before the private investigator made peace with the Apaches.
(Courtesy Glenn Magill)

The pit above the tunnel. Was this the fabled
Lost Dutchman Mine? *(Courtesy Glenn Magill)*

Bill Young in the cemetery in Arizpe, Sonora, Mexico, looking
for Peralta graves. *(Courtesy Glenn Magill)*

A warning? A copperhead snake killed just outside Magill's motel room in Apache Junction, Arizona. The puzzler: copperheads are not native to Arizona. *(Courtesy Glenn Magill)*

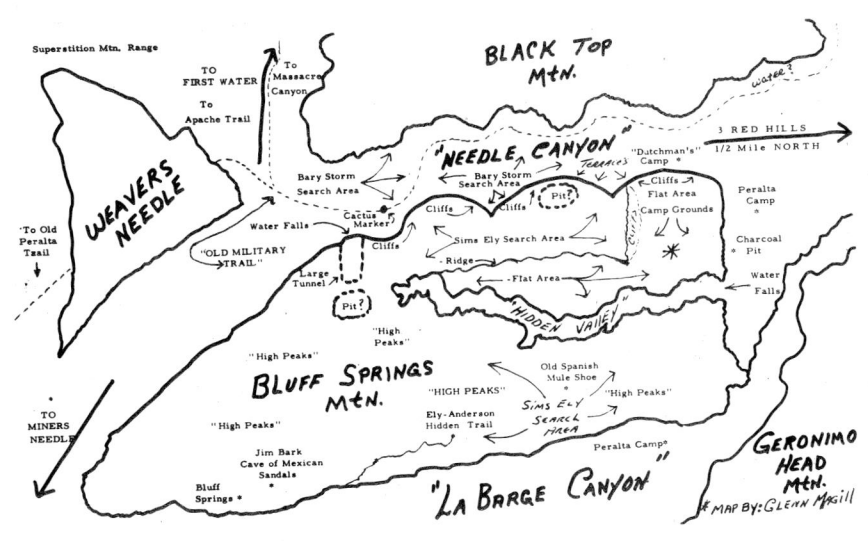

MAP D
Glenn Magill's own map of the key landmarks in the Lost Dutchman Mine search. *(Courtesy Glenn Magill)*

CHAPTER 7

An Insurance Policy

ADOLPH RUTH, James Cravey, Guy "Hematite" Frink, Dr. John Burns, Joseph Kelley, Martin Zywotho, Franz Harrer, William Richard Harvey, Hilmer Bohen, Walter Mowry, and Jay Clapp were all dead for one reason—they had chosen to go into the Superstitions alone.

Now that he had the maps, Magill was not about to repeat their mistake. In entering the mountains this time he wanted a strong force, one not only equipped to handle any emergency that might arise, but whose very number and obvious preparation—i.e., arms—would discourage interference.

Stanley Fernández and an indeterminate number of others were dead because of their choice of partners. Those twisted mountains did strange things to men's minds. Barry Storm had brought in a geologist on one of his hunts; even before the first glimpse of "color," the man was plotting to eliminate him.

(Storm had marched him out at gunpoint.) Magill wanted to select carefully each member of the expedition.

This resurrected an old problem. With a single exception, there was no one with whom he could frankly discuss the Dutchman search.

Now, more than ever, he felt the loss of the Denver attorney. Could he "sell" the Dutchman to others? Magill was not sure.

The single exception was Charles Rhoades.

Rhoades was a quiet, thoughtful man in his early fifties. As a barnstorming young mail pilot, he had conceived an item so essential as to become standard equipment on every plane that took to the air. This invention had earned him not only considerable money but also a healthy amount of kidding, since his creation was the "Sick-Sac." After patenting the sack and setting up a company to manufacture it, he had decided to spend the rest of his life doing things that interested him. He had mined a bit, worked in the oil fields, even hunted (unsuccessfully) for the loot of the James gang. His greatest interest was metaphysics, however, particularly the philosophy of the psychic Edgar Cayce. As an outgrowth of this latter interest, Rhoades had set up the New Age Center in Oklahoma City, where visiting lecturers spoke on subjects ranging from hypnotism to yoga to flying saucers.

Rhoades was not a "true believer," however, rather the opposite, a man with an inquiring mind. He and Magill had been close friends for more than five years, and he was the one person with whom Magill could discuss the Dutchman without fear of ridicule. Charley listened, said nothing until all the evidence had been presented, asked a few pointed questions, and when asked for an opinion—but not before—said frankly what he thought. A number of Magill's pet theories had stopped right here.

As a friend in whom he could place complete trust, Magill wanted Charley in. There was another reason for including him. He was determined that everyone who took part in the expedition must contribute something. Rhoades had a "pilot's eye." He could spot landmarks in maps and photographs that even Magill, for all his investigative background, could not see.

Rhoades asked for a few days to consider the proposition. Magill had anticipated this and was prepared to wait. The wait was not that long, however; Magill received his answer that night.

Charles Rhoades became the first partner.

Baker Looney was the second.

Short, wiry, energetic, in his mid-twenties, Looney was Magill's chief assistant in the detective agency. The Dutchman did not come as a complete surprise to him. Having been in and out of Magill's office at every hour of the day and night, he had overheard enough telephone conversations to figure out what his boss was up to. Magill would have been disappointed had Baker not guessed, inasmuch as observation was the keystone of investigative training.

Magill told him about the maps.

"When do we leave?" was Baker's quick reply.

Magill wanted six men in the group. The figure wasn't arbitrarily chosen. During his last telephone call to Albuquerque, Crandall had warned that if he planned to go into the mountains any time in the near future he should proceed cautiously, as there were "six guns" on Black Top Mountain. Since Magill would be conducting his search on the cliffs of Bluff Springs Mountain, directly across Needle Canyon and well within the range of high-powered rifles, he wanted at least equal odds. With six men, if there was an accident—if one man fell and broke his leg, for example—two men could carry him out while the others continued the work. A larger group would be difficult to manage.

For all their virtues, both Charley and Baker were "lightweights"; neither weighed over 150 pounds. Anticipating what lay ahead, Magill knew he needed muscle.

It's possible that sometime, somewhere, a miner merely spotted gold on the ground, stooped down and picked it up, and made his fortune. If so, it was the exception that proved the rule, for mining has always been one of the hardest, most backbreaking types of work devised by man. Familiar with the tortured slopes of Bluff Springs Mountain, where winds were often strong enough to push a man over the precipice, Magill knew he would need at least one man who feared nothing, to whom strenuous physical labor was commonplace.

He had such a man in mind.

For the past several months Magill had been in process of building a vacation cabin at Twin Lakes Sports Club, in the mountains near Oklahoma City. The man in charge of construction was a handsome, rugged six-footer named Andy Vloedman. Watching him at work, digging foundations, carrying timbers, laying bricks, Magill had been amazed at his capacity for work. Andy was, to use a cliché, the type of man who worked hard, played hard, and drank his whiskey straight. Magill felt he would be a definite asset to the expedition.

Approaching Charley and Baker had been relatively easy, for both men had some background knowledge of the project and Magill's own approach to it. He had to approach Vloedman cold. Working alongside him one day, Magill waited for the psychological moment, when they broke for a beer, then asked: Had he ever heard of the Lost Dutchman Mine? Andy had; he'd always thought that he just might go look for it someday.

With this opening, Magill plunged into his tale. From the first, Andy's reaction was obvious. The whole thing greatly appealed to his sense of adventure.

"You think you can find this mine?" Andy interrupted.

"I know I can," Magill asserted.

"Then why are we sitting here on our duffs?"

Magill had anticipated a few refusals. An opposite problem now arose. Andy and Charley each wanted to invite a friend.

The Rhoadeses had a young boarder, Carl Lee, whom Charley and his wife had befriended. Carl was only nineteen and Charley wanted him to come along for the experience. Magill had met Carl and been amused by his quick wit, but he postponed a definite answer.

Magill knew Andy's friend, Jim Miller,* a little better, since he had helped Andy work on the cabin several weekends. Though Andy was large, Jim nevertheless looked like a giant beside him. Six-six, in his early thirties, he weighed over two hundred pounds and seemed to be all muscle and bone.

There was much to be said for Miller's participation. Magill had watched Jim and Andy working together; they made an excellent team. Also, he had liked Jim from the moment he saw him. And there was another reason. One look at Jim, Magill knew, and the six armed prospectors on Black Top would have second thoughts before interfering with the group.

On the other hand, he knew neither Carl nor Jim well enough to predict their reaction under fire. He was extremely reluctant to take along anyone whose conduct in a moment of stress could not be predicted. The Superstitions had a way of creating such moments, repeatedly.

* "Jim Miller" is an alias. For personal reasons, connected with his business, one of the men has requested that his name not be used, and the author has complied with his request.

He told Andy to say nothing to Jim until he had given the matter further thought. He had already cautioned Charley and Baker about the need for complete secrecy.

Magill had almost decided to postpone the trip for several months.

A couple of others who had been approached couldn't get away from their jobs for at least that long. And, to date, they were without financing. Neither Magill nor any of the other men was wealthy. All had jobs and responsibilities, and with the exception of Carl Lee, families to support.

As far as Magill's own work was concerned, the expedition couldn't have come at a worse time.

He had recently been elected president of the Oklahoma Association of Private Detectives. Shortly before this, he had received the Tenth Annual Award of the International Investigator's Society for Outstanding Service in the Public Interest, in recognition of his charity work in locating missing persons in welfare cases; as usual, a number of these cases were pending. Also, he had recently been the first private detective in the United States to be appointed by a Federal Court to conduct an investigation in behalf of an indigent, under the new Supreme Court ruling that those unable to afford such aid were entitled to it by law. In addition, his regular work load at this time was abnormally heavy, thanks to Tweetie Pie.

It is probable that private detectives rank second only to newspapers as magnets for crackpots. Too, policemen seem to take special delight in passing on "difficult cases" to the "private eyes." One such case, bequeathed to Magill by a "friend" on the Oklahoma City force, was a spinster lady bothered by a man from Mars who materialized in her bedroom each night. The problem wasn't that he tried to rape her, rather the opposite.

Over the years Magill had become adept at fending off such callers, at the same time trying his best not to offend them. At first he had planned to fend off the case of Tweetie Pie.

The woman had come to him in hysterics. She was desperate; the police couldn't help her. Her closest and dearest friend, the only person she really loved, had disappeared.

Magill asked her to describe her friend.

Tweetie Pie was yellow, she said, about three inches tall, and——

Had it not been for the woman's obvious discomfort, Magill would have had trouble keeping a straight face. Tweetie Pie, she finally explained, was a pet parakeet who had flown out the window ten days ago and not returned.

Magill had recovered a number of missing and stolen animals, but never a parakeet. Since the bird had been missing more than a week and could be presumed to be less than a creature of the wilds, Magill knew the chance of finding it, alive or dead, was extremely remote. It was a ridiculous assignment, but the more Magill thought about it, the more it became a personal challenge. He took the case. The sight of Magill and his operatives walking the streets of Oklahoma City, calling up to the trees, "Tweetie Pie, Tweetie Pie," must have mystified more than a few Sooners.

He had found Tweetie Pie, however, alive and well in a tree only a block from home and had been paid a ridiculous fee for his efforts. The woman was so grateful, in fact, that she told the newspapers about it. Within days Magill was barraged with calls from most of the fifty states. "If you're so good at finding dumb animals," one woman had said, "maybe you can find my husband. He's been missing thirteen years."

While only a small portion of the calls actually developed into assignments, they added considerably to the confusion of Magill's never very quiet life.

Magill had almost decided to postpone the trip to a less hectic time—after all, the mine had been safely lost for seventy-five years—when he received a call from Dr. Ruth.

Ruth called early one evening to inform Magill that a prospector named Peck, who had been tracking down the Dutchman for several years, had called on him and asked if his father had made copies of the maps. Ruth had confirmed his having done so and, inasmuch as he had already given copies to Magill, felt that he should accord Peck the same courtesy.

He could put off delivery of the maps for a couple of weeks, however, which would give Magill that much head start.

Magill had not anticipated this kind of competition. While it seemed unlikely that Peck would be able to decipher the maps immediately on receipt, Magill couldn't risk that possibility. All he knew for sure was that he had two weeks in which to find the mine. Scheduling a meeting in his office that evening, he asked Andy and Charley to bring Jim and Carl along.

Magill did not minimize the hardships or the risks, nor did he inflate hopes as to what they might find. His approach was decidedly pessimistic. He didn't want anyone to claim later that he had been lured along under false pretenses.

All he could promise with any assurance, he told them, was that if the clues on the map checked out—if they could find the water hole, the cave with the house, the tunnel, and other landmarks—then he should be able to direct them to the spot where the pit should be.

He used the phrase "should be" advisedly. A single earthquake or landslide could have covered it with tons of rocks.

Even discounting the earthquake possibility, the likelihood of their finding a mine open and ready to be worked was remote. If it was true, as the Apaches claimed, that they had filled in and disguised the mine, then, even were they lucky enough to find the exact spot, they might have to dig through some thirty feet of rock and dirt before reaching the vein.

Even then there was no assurance they would find gold. There was one bothersome thing about the Dutchman's story. Jacob Waltz had stopped working the mine in 1884, seven years before he died. He may have already had more gold than he could use. He may have feared the Apaches. He may have felt too old to continue. It was also possible that the vein had run out, that there was no more gold. Despite the glittering legend, the Lost Dutchman Mine could very well prove to be a dry shaft.

He could not promise them one ounce of gold, only a very rough and rugged trip beset with dangers and hazards.

In much the same way as Crandall had instructed him, Magill told them of what they could expect to encounter. He warned them that while most prospectors in the Superstitions minded their own business and expected others to do likewise, there were a few—touched by the sun perhaps or simply driven mad by the mountains—who believed that they had a claim on the Lost Dutchman Mine simply by virtue of having spent so much time in quest of it. Such men, Magill believed, were probably responsible for most of the Superstition murders.

These murders, he stressed, had increased in number over recent years.

His attempt to dampen their enthusiasm was ineffective. They wanted to leave that night.

Magill had a lawyer draw up a contract, setting forth terms of the search.

Each of the six—Magill, Rhoades, Looney, Vloedman, Miller, and Lee—would absorb an equal share of the trip expenses. In return, if anything of monetary value was found, each would receive an equal share.

E*

Magill knew he could set any terms he desired. He could just as easily—without a single complaint—have given each of the men 10 percent, keeping the remaining 50 percent for himself. He felt, however, that if he was asking them to assume the risks of the search—of which none of them was more than vaguely aware—they should share equally in any reward. Too, if they were equal partners, while this might not eliminate greed, it would at least reduce the likelihood of discord born of envy.

For himself, Magill reserved, in addition to his one-sixth, only three things: the right to act as spokesman for the group; all publicity rights to the story; and the first $5,000 from any monies recovered, as token reimbursement for expenses already incurred in the search.

There were two more interesting paragraphs in the contract:

One provided that should any member of the group in any way betray the others he would forfeit his share.

The other provided that should any one of them die—of whatever cause, natural or otherwise—his share would automatically go to his heirs at law. Under no circumstances would it accrue to any of the partners.

Magill had, in effect, drawn up what amounted to an insurance policy.

To maintain secrecy, all supplies, including two pack mules, were purchased in Oklahoma City. In addition to food, bedrolls, tools, dynamite, snake-bite kits, and other necessities, they purchased a half-dozen high-powered rifles, an equal number of side arms, and enough ammunition to hold off not only a few crazed prospectors but a whole tribe of Apaches.

The mules and supplies were loaded into the back of a large truck. Two of the men rode in the cab; the others followed by car. They left Oklahoma City at noon on Saturday, April 23, 1966.

CHAPTER 8

The Tunnel and the Pit

DUE TO a late start, coupled with car trouble en route, the group did not reach Peralta 1 Camp until Sunday afternoon.

There are two major entrances to the Superstitions: First Water, located on the west side of the mountains, near Goldfield; and Peralta 1, on the south side of the range, along the Old Peralta Road to Mexico. Magill chose the latter as starting point for this trip in, hoping to attract less attention.

He did so despite a rumor that both camps were under the constant surveillance of a group of men from a town close by. Object: robbery and/or murder.

This, some contended, was the simple explanation for the Superstition deaths.

One curious fact concerning the slayings was often cited as partial support for this theory: none of the victims was a local man. It was as if each had been carefully chosen to avoid more than a routine inquest.

In studying these deaths, however, Magill had discovered another interesting fact. In almost every case, when the body was finally located, the victim's money was found to be intact. But as Dobie has observed, facts have no business getting in the way of a good story.

The men saw no one.* But there were several locked cars nearby, and Charley noticed something odd about them. They had been backed up so that their rear ends ran snug into the side of the mountain—making it impossible for anyone to read their license plates. Obviously people entering the Superstitions were not anxious to be identified.

By the time the truck was unloaded and the gear assembled, the mountains were casting long shadows. It was decided to postpone the trip into the interior until the following morning. In cinching up the mules, they had encountered an unexpected problem. Although the mules had been sold to them as "trailwise," it was all too apparent that one, whom they promptly dubbed Satan, had never been ridden.

There was a corral in the area, built by the Dons Club of Phoenix for their annual trek. While Charley cooked supper, the others took turns breaking in Satan.

Andy was first to try, sailing about five feet into the air, then coming down hard on his hunkers. When Satan let out a laughing bray and Andy arose minus the seat of his pants, Carl Lee couldn't resist an appropriate remark.

From Andy's look at Carl, as he dusted off his behind and remounted, it was obvious Satan wasn't the only one he wanted to break. It had already become apparent that Carl Lee's brand of humor was going to pall quite soon.

Satan's stubbornness disappeared faster. By early evening

---

* They were not unobserved, however. As they would later learn, word reached Apache Junction that evening that a small army had invaded the Superstitions.

Andy, with Jim as chief alternate, had managed to make Satan almost as docile as his companion, Pauline.

That night the men were initiated into some other facets of the mountains.

Jim rolled out his bedroll and started to slide in, only to discover that the spot he had chosen was already occupied—by a bed of huge centipedes.

The other incident remains unexplained.

In unpacking, the men had been unable to find a coal oil lantern purchased especially for the trip; finally, after much harried searching, they assumed it had been left behind. In the middle of the night, Jim was awakened by an eerie light. Standing between two of the bedrolls, burning brightly, was the lantern.

The next morning Carl Lee was accused of having engineered a practical joke. Not only did he deny it, he appeared even more shaken than the others.

When, shortly after dawn, they set off up the trail, the men were, without exception, badly unnerved.

For their route Magill had chosen the old tortuous horseback trail once used by the Peraltas. As the sun rose higher and the trail grew rougher, the distance between the leadman, Baker, and the tail, Charley, grew, until their only resemblance to an army was to one in rout. At the same time, more and more equipment mysteriously disappeared from the backs of the men to reappear on those of the mules. All held on to their weapons, however, except Charley, who, against all arguments, had refused to carry a gun. His philosophy was simple: if he didn't have one, he wouldn't be tempted to use it.

There's something about those mountains, Crandall had once

told Magill, that turns the best organized team into a collection of individuals.

At many points the trail was so narrow the burros couldn't pass without their packs rubbing the rocks. This would loosen the straps, causing packs to shift, then slide under the bellies of the animals. In one tight squeeze several water jugs were broken. Other places the trail rose several hundred feet off the desert floor and narrowed to ledges less than two feet wide. Andy and Jim had done their work well, however, for Satan, like Pauline, never missed a step.

Although it was only April, by mid-morning the temperature was into the nineties, the heat seeming to exude from the rocks as much as the sky, which remained cloudless. They saw no rattlers, though occasionally they heard them, the mules shying jerkily. There was, they soon learned, when they stopped for breaks, a scorpion under almost every rock they moved. They stopped moving rocks.

At noon they stopped briefly to eat sandwiches, prepared in advance, then pushed on toward Weaver's Needle. About a mile farther up the trail they discovered that the watering can for the mules had been left behind; Carl Lee volunteered to go back for it.

If you encounter any trouble, he was instructed, fire your pistol three times.

Less than an hour later they heard three gunshots, followed by Carl's hoarse cry. Minutes later he came running up the trail, panting so hard he could barely speak.

"Someone's following us!" he gasped.

"If this is a joke——" Andy started.

"No," he sobbed. "I swear it's the truth!"

Doubling back, he pointed to the evidence—a pair of tracks crossing theirs. The prints were clear, but very odd. From their distinctive tread, it was obvious they had been made by tennis shoes, unlikely footwear for mountain use.

That night, when they camped in Needle Canyon not far from the Dutchman's campsite, they posted a guard, rotated on two-hour watch until morning.

After breakfast, Charley and Carl were delegated to take charge of the camp, while the others paired off and "cut for sign."

Magill had located the first clue on the map, the water hole in Needle Canyon, before the group left Oklahoma City. It had served as his source of water on a previous trip.

Comparing the map with photographs and aided by the *Arizona Republic* description published at the time the archeological expedition found Ruth's skull, he had also determined that Black Top Mesa, a spur of the mountain, was probably the site of the next clue. Moving out over the slopes of the mesa, ever conscious of the six guns in the rocks above, even though they had not yet seen them, the men began looking for the Caverna con Casa.

After several hours' search, they found it. It was exactly where it appeared on the map, a small natural cave extending only a few feet back into the mountain. In its entrance were several large stone blocks, the remains of what had once been a stone house.

Within sight of this landmark Adolph Ruth had died.

If the map was accurate, the tunnel should be almost directly opposite the cave, across Needle Canyon, on the cliffs on the westerly side of Bluff Springs Mountain.

And the mine should be just a short distance above it.

Through binoculars they studied the craggy west face of Bluff Springs, looking for some sign of the tunnel. There was nothing that even faintly resembled it.

According to an 1895 newspaper account, the tunnel was partially hidden by trees. They could not see even a single tree.

Slowly they worked back down to the floor of Needle Canyon, then began their ascent of the opposite side.

"The mine is in awful rough country" Jacob Waltz told Julia Thomas and Reiney Petrasch, "so rough that you can be right at the mine without seeing it."

Looking up at the almost perpendicular cliffs, "awful rough" seemed like gross understatement.

"Are you sure this is the right mountain?" one of the men asked. "Couldn't it maybe be another a little flatter?"

They encountered difficulties immediately. The climb was nearly straight up. Each foothold had to be tested to determine whether it could bear a man's weight. Before reaching to the ledge above for a handhold, it had to be probed gingerly with a stick, to make sure it wasn't already occupied by snakes. Yet while the others proceeded slowly and cautiously, Baker scampered. Watching him move agilely up the sheer cliffs, leaping across crevices, hanging from ledges so narrow they couldn't be seen from below, the others thought he resembled a monkey: they dubbed him official mascot of the expedition.

Mrs. Barkley had once told Magill that she did not believe the mountains were in themselves evil, but rather that there was something here that magnified and accentuated the qualities already inside a man. If true, the quality in Baker that the mountain enhanced was curiosity. He peered into every hole. He couldn't pass a large rock without looking behind to see what it hid.

He was about a dozen yards from them, above and to their left, when he began sliding. He fell slowly at first, from one ledge to another, hitting the rocks so sharply they ripped off his waterbag. As he threw his arms around a boulder and hung on, the scene continued to play itself out as if in slow motion—the bag taking an infinite amount of time to reach the canyon floor, two hundred feet below. Then, while the others watched in horror, unable to help, Baker lost his grip and began sliding again, picking up momentum, falling some twenty feet before his body dropped out of sight behind a small grove of trees.

The trees, located in a narrow ravine, had escaped notice earlier. With agonizing slowness, they worked their way toward them now, not calling out Baker's name for fear there would be no reply.

Andy was first to reach the thicket. He found Baker sitting on a stump, grinning and smoking a cigarette. Miraculously, there wasn't a bruise on him, though his cigarettes had been somewhat crushed.

"I'll be God damned," Andy gasped. But he was looking beyond Baker, not at him. There, completely hidden by the trees, was the mouth of a cave. Looking inside, he could see that it was easily thirty feet high and that, sloping upward, it extended some sixty-five feet back into Bluff Springs Mountain.

The Peralta map showed a tunnel.

"Don Miguel's father had started a tunnel in the hillside, down below," the Dutchman said. "It pointed straight toward where the ore would lie, deeper down."

"On the hillside below the mine there was the portal to a tunnel," Dearing told Brown. "Through the opening I could see that the tunnel pointed toward the pit."

Although the site corresponded to the map, and the floor slanted upward toward where the pit should be, just as both men had described it, Magill's first reaction was disappointment. This was a cave, not a tunnel.

Earlier he had cautioned the men about twisting clues to fit the find. "The only thing that separates us from the other searchers," he had said, "is the map. We've got to stick to it, no matter how tempting other prospects may be."

"It *is* a tunnel," Jim yelled from deep inside. "Come look."

The tunnel began at the back of the cave and extended some 10 feet straight into the rock.

It made sense. Why go to the trouble of digging a whole tunnel when nature had provided an excellent start? Too, the inked-in depiction on the Peralta map was a near-perfect likeness of the cave's shape.

"One clue down," someone said.

"And here's another."

Sims Ely and Jim Bark had spent considerable time trying to track down the source of timbers used as ladders in the pit. The only tree stumps they had found were miles from this area, over terrain much too rough for hauling. Yet here, where Baker had been sitting, was a whole row of stumps.

If this was the tunnel, they realized almost simultaneously, then the mine should be directly above it!

Excitedly, they began to look for a way to scale the sheer rock wall.

Back at camp, Charley was tending the fire when he noticed a solitary figure on the lower slopes of Bluff Springs Mountain, at just about the point where the mountain curved to the east. At first he thought it was one of their party, somehow separated from the others. Looking through binoculars, however, he saw that the man was middle-aged and heavily bearded, a stranger. He appeared to be stringing wire along the ground.

As Charley watched, he stopped and fastened it to a black box. At the same time, he moved behind a large boulder and knelt down, his arms straight out in front of him.

It couldn't be, Charley thought, but he had seen enough mining to know better. *It was a dynamite plunger!* Before Charley could yell the man pushed it down.

The explosion seemed to jar the whole mountain.

As the men dove for cover—some into the cave, others behind the trees—a shower of rocks came down, followed by a half-dozen large boulders that flew over them, sheering the tops of the trees, rumbling on down the cliffs.

For several minutes the men lay still, waiting for the rockslide to stop. Fortunately no one had been hit. Then Andy spotted the man and, standing, framed him in the scope of his rifle.

The man saw Andy too and began frantically to wave his arms. Andy lowered the gun, but kept it aimed in the man's general direction.

It took nearly a quarter of an hour for the men to work their way back down the mountain to where the man was waiting. Long before they had reached him, however, he was shouting apologies. It was an accident; he hadn't realized that anyone else was in the area.

Only when he stuck out his hand to introduce himself did they replace the safeties on their guns.

His name was Al Morrow, he said. He had been prospecting in the Superstitions for twelve years and for the past several months had been working on the other side of Bluff Springs Mountain. He hadn't meant to scare them—in fact, he didn't know anyone was in the vicinity. He had planted the charge on the other side of the mountain, near the base; apparently it had triggered a slide of loose rock from above.

"You could have killed us, you know," Baker said. "It's lucky we had the cave to duck into."

"Cave?"

"The one behind the trees," Baker ventured, and then fell silent abruptly when Andy kicked him surreptitiously.

"I don't know of any trees or cave around here." Morrow looked puzzled.

On previous trips Magill had taken dozens of photos of Bluff Springs Mountain, which he had magnified and studied closely. Yet he too had never noticed the trees. The way the ravine closed around them, they were almost hidden from view from the canyon below.

Morrow, to make amends, invited them to his camp for coffee. Like most solitary prospectors, he was friendly but cautious. When he volunteered information he managed to receive more than he gave. He was likable enough, however, and obviously hungry for human companionship. While the water was boiling, he showed them his diggings, located a short distance from his camp. No one asked if he had found any gold, and Morrow didn't say. He also pointed out the remains of another stone house nearby. There were faint markings on two of the stone blocks. On one was chiseled the figures "1761," on the other "1847."

If the figures were dates, the first was carved during the time of the Jesuits, six years before their expulsion; the latter, during the time of the Peraltas.

Of course, it was possible, despite their faintness and weatherworn look, that they had been carved at a later date. It was also possible that they weren't meant to be dates, but symbols or signs.

Although Morrow obviously had his own explanation of their meaning, he kept it to himself.

There were many such oddities in the Superstitions. Indian pictographs in Hieroglyphic Canyon in which the figure of a man with an ore sack on his back was clearly evident; giant saguaro cacti with strange markings. There were, Magill realized, more than enough clues for everyone. Morrow was welcome to his.

The coffee was good and the parting almost cordial, the men promising to bring Morrow a carton of cigarettes on their next trip in. They were about equally divided as to whether the blasting was accidental or a "friendly warning."

Leaving Morrow, the men returned to camp to plan their strategy.

The cliff above the tunnel was unscalable, at least with their limited gear. If there had once been easy access between the mine and the tunnel, rock slides had removed it long ago, leaving a sheer face, extending upward for some thirty feet. With ropes they could make it, but first someone would have to go to the top of the mountain and work his way down.

Moreover, Magill was convinced that neither the Peraltas nor the Dutchman had reached the mine by the route they had followed, which was directly up from the canyon floor.

For one thing, it was in open sight of anyone who might be watching; the Dutchman had been much more cautious. For another, it was too steep for mules; and the Peraltas had hobbled their mules *on top* of Bluff Springs Mountain, in the hidden valley. Third, in describing how he and his partner had spotted the two Mexicans they thought to be Apaches, Waltz had told of climbing onto a ridge, then looking down at the mine.

Obviously there must be another means of access to the mine, from above. From what they could see from below, the tunnel was located in a ravine formed by a split in the top of the mountain. They would have to locate the start of the ravine, then follow it down.

How far above the tunnel was the pit or mine?

There was disagreement on this point, due entirely to the cryptic last words of Adolph Ruth: "About 200 feet across from cave."

Magill was not at all sure what Ruth meant. If by "cave" he

was referring to the Caverna con Casa on Black Top, then he couldn't have meant the distance across Needle Canyon to the tunnel on Bluff Springs, for this was obviously a great deal farther.

That the tunnel on Bluff Springs was also a cave opened other possibilities. It was the majority opinion of the group—in which Magill did not concur—that Ruth was indicating the distance between the tunnel and the pit. But Ruth had written "200 feet *across* from cave," not *"up* from cave." Also Magill was not convinced that Adolph Ruth had never set foot on Bluff Springs Mountain. Once at the site, it seemed incredible to him that the aged Ruth, with his game leg, could have made the arduous climb to the tunnel, then managed to find a way to the pit above it.

There was still more conclusive evidence. Ruth's skeleton and effects had been found on Black Top, within sight of the first clue, the Caverna con Casa.

From what he now knew, Magill tried to recreate the scene. It was hypothetical, yet possible, that the "200 feet across from cave" might indicate something Ruth had found on Black Top, quite possibly the old mine mentioned in the *Arizona Republic* article, which showed signs of recent working. Whoever had followed him couldn't have known that this was a side trip, however, thereby deducing Ruth had actually found the Lost Dutchman. If so, he must have discovered his error soon after killing Ruth. He would then have had another bitter surprise—the realization that the map was useless unless one knew how to interpret it.

And the *Veni, vidi, vici?* Mightn't Ruth have penned that on discovering the cave was exactly where the map showed it to be?

Magill felt that the others were wrong about the two hundred feet. For the moment, however, it seemed a moot point. The problem now was reaching the top of Bluff Springs Mountain.

Magill had successfully scaled it on his last trip, but it had been a rugged, dangerous climb requiring the better part of a day. To accomplish it, they would have to leave the mules and most of their gear below, since rockslides had destroyed the lower portions of the path. Although Magill felt confident that the water holes atop Bluff Springs provided fresh water year round, he couldn't be absolutely sure. For their own safety they couldn't gamble on it. They would have to take enough water and supplies to cover their basic needs.

It was Charley who finally advanced a solution.

While the others remained camped in Needle Canyon, Magill and Charley luxuriated guiltily on the comfortable beds of the Superstition Inn at Apache Junction, sipping bourbon and waiting for a telephone call.

Earlier Charley had recalled that a one-time flying buddy now lived somewhere in the Phoenix area. When they reached Apache Junction, he had made several telephone calls, finally locating the friend and explaining their problem. They were in need of a helicopter pilot willing to bootleg them into the Superstitions; did he know of such a man?

He knew someone he thought might be willing to risk it.

Finally, after several hours' waiting, the helicopter pilot called. Magill talked to him.

Doing a favor for a friend of a friend was one thing, he explained; however, breaking the law was another. He would be willing to risk it, he said, but only on certain conditions.

The rate would be seventy-five dollars an hour. It was a small copter and he would be able to take in only one man and a limited amount of supplies per trip. Too, since the Superstitions were located in the Tonto National Forest, which was a national wilderness area, it was illegal for a motorized vehicle to enter. To remain on the technical side of the law, he wouldn't be able to set the copter down but would have to hover a foot or two aboveground while the man jumped out and unloaded supplies.

This was, he admitted, not without its dangers, but it was a necessary condition.

The rate was steep, and with six men plus water, food, supplies, and equipment could run into a sizable figure. Yet there was no alternative. Although Magill was anxious to leave before dawn, the pilot refused to leave until afternoon. There was less chance of being spotted by rangers at that time.

Magill and Charley arranged to meet the pilot at an isolated spot near the edge of the Superstitions at twelve the following day.

About seven the next morning Magill and Charley were having breakfast in the coffee shop when Baker stumbled in, literally. His clothing was torn, his hair matted, his whole body so covered with dirt from head to foot he was barely recognizable. He was also so exhausted it was some minutes before he could speak.

He had set out late the previous afternoon to join them, but taking what he thought would be a shortcut, had become trapped on a ledge, where he spent most of the night.

Yet, tired as he was, he could barely conceal his excitement. They had made two discoveries.

They had found the huge stone face the Dutchman said looked up to his mine. Only it wasn't looking anywhere now, but was lying on its side in Needle Canyon, where it had apparently been rolled from the mountain above. The Apache tale was true.

Returning to the tunnel and examining it more carefully, they had also found, on the right-hand wall of the cave, a faint outline of what appeared to be a stone door. It was partly covered with rocks, but some of these had apparently fallen and rolled out of the tunnel, leaving the top of the door exposed. In tapping the wall around the outline they got a solid sound. In tapping the door—which they were convinced it was—there was a decidedly hollow echo.

Could this be the hiding place of the Jesuit treasure? Baker wondered.

Still another possibility had occurred to Magill.

Geronimo's cave was in a sacred place, by a hidden valley, near water, Goochie had told Magill. The water fell over the face of the mountain, making a waterfall that hid the cave.

The ravine above the tunnel, Magill realized, formed a natural waterfall. Although he had never seen this area during a rain, the trees themselves were proof that an adequate amount of water reached the area.

Was the cave on Bluff Springs Mountain also the Apache ceremonial cave?

This might explain why the Peraltas had never completed their tunnel.

"There's something spooky about that place," Baker said.

"What do you mean 'spooky'?"

"I don't know. You just get an odd feeling. None of us want to work around there any more than we have to."

Despite Baker's caution—perhaps in part because of it—Magill was anxious to spend more time exploring the tunnel area. But arrangements for the helicopter had already been made.

"Oh, we found one more thing," Baker said just as his breakfast arrived. "More of those tennis-shoe tracks."

After breakfast they returned to their room, Baker dropping exhausted onto one of the beds.

There were sliding glass doors along one side of the room, opening onto a patio and affording a clear view of the Superstition palisades. Magill pulled back the curtains and slid open the door, intending to step out for some air.

The sun was bright, however, and momentarily blinded him, causing him to hesitate a minute in the doorway. When his eyes adjusted to the glare, he quickly stepped back inside and slammed the door shut.

"What's the matter?" Charley asked. Magill's hands were shaking; perspiration had broken out on his forehead.

He pointed through the glass. On the patio, less than two feet from where Magill had been standing, was a large snake, poised and ready to strike.

While Charley called the motel manager, Magill watched the snake uncoil itself and slither away. Within minutes the manager arrived with a gardener and hoe; the snake was quickly decapitated. Measuring nearly three feet in length, it was easily identifiable from its markings as a copperhead.

"Snakes have *never* come this close to the inn before," the manager said to Magill indignantly, as if accusing him of having brought it.

Magill suspected there might be at least a half-truth in the charge—that someone had placed it there. He went outside to look around.

In crawling from the desert floor to the patio, the snake should have left tracks. In their excitement, they had obscured any tracks in the immediate area but farther out there should be some. Magill couldn't find any.

And why would the snake have chosen to crawl toward the cement patio, when there was no shade here?

One other fact was even more puzzling. Copperheads are not indigenous to Arizona.

While Baker returned to bed, the patio door securely locked and the room itself thoroughly searched, Magill and Charley shopped in Apache Junction for additional supplies. In one of the clothing stores Magill made a casual inquiry: "Do you sell many tennis shoes?"

The Killer Mountains 145

"Can't keep them in stock," the storekeeper replied. "Course most people don't know this, but sometime ago the Indians discovered that to make mocassins takes more time than they are worth. Oh, they still make them—for the tourists. Only when they're off by themselves they prefer cheaper and more durable footwear. Now every time I get a shipment of tennis shoes the Apaches on the San Carlos Reservation buy me out."

Involuntarily Magill shivered. He had just remembered something.

"You from out of state?" the storekeeper asked.

Magill admitted that he was.

"Then you probably may not know it," he said proudly, "but there are only three Apache reservations in the United States, and two of them, San Carlos and White Mountain, are right here in this area. Why, there must be 100,000 Apaches in Arizona, give or take a few."

It was not exactly what Magill wanted to hear, inasmuch as he had just recalled that Apaches had a custom of sending snakes to their enemies, as warning.

"If you look through the binoculars, right up there between those rocks," Andy said, "you can see them. They're making no effort to remain hidden."

Magill focused his binoculars on a spot about halfway up the slope of Black Top Mountain. Although it was late afternoon, and Needle Canyon was already partly in shadow, there was still enough light on the mountainside to clearly highlight the two figures in detail. They were Apaches. Although their clothing was western, their hair was long and braided, in the old fashion. They sat there, almost as immobile as the rocks, but in clear view, looking directly across canyon at the activities atop Bluff Springs.

Magill was not too surprised. He was almost relieved, as the Indians were real, not a figment of imagination. Earlier that afternoon, after being set down by the helicopter, he had heard an owl hoot. In the Old West, such a sound would have sent a pioneer running for his gun. Owls don't hoot during the daytime; Apaches do. It is their traditional warning.

As an investigator Magill recognized the human tendency to try to form a meaningful pattern from totally unrelated events. Altogether there were four separate incidents—the tennis-shoe tracks, the snake, the owl hoot, the two solitary watchers. There might be a simple, unconnected explanation for each. Personally, Magill thought not. It was too much coincidence in one package.

He was sure of only one thing. If the tennis-shoe tracks did belong to the Apaches, they were meant to be seen. Many generations had passed since the days of Mangus Colorado, Cochise, Victorio, Nana, and Geronimo. But he could not believe their descendants had lost their ability for skillful tracking.

The open presence of the two Indians gave additional confirmation. Had they wanted to watch secretly, they could have done so quite easily. Yet they sat in plain view, as if wanting to be noticed.

The possibility they were in the vicinity of the sacred ground and were being warned of it seemed very real.

There was a large flat area on the top of Bluff Springs, near the north end. It was here Magill had directed the pilot to set down the men and supplies. And here, under a large overhanging ledge, they established base camp. It was nearly two miles from the spot they wanted to explore, the cliffs on the southwest corner of the mountain, but this was as much asset as liability, at least as far as secrecy was concerned, since the pilot would not be able to pinpoint the exact area of their explorations.

Only essential supplies had been ferried to the top of the mountain. The balance had been left in Needle Canyon, together with the mules, which had been supplied with adequate water and feed. Still, the whole operation had taken eight hours, costing them $600.

Although it was nearly dark, some of the men wanted to start looking for the pit immediately, but wiser counsel prevailed. The first thing, Magill decided, was to see if there was still water in the hidden valley.

"We don't have to go that far," Charley said. "There's water closer than that."

"How do you know?" Bob asked.

"I have a nose for it," Charley modestly admitted. To their amazement, he led them straight to a catch basin of clear, fresh water, located only a short distance from their campsite. Earlier there had been considerable good-natured ribbing about Charley's alleged psychic powers. It ceased abruptly.

That evening after dinner—Charley had proven himself possessed of an even greater power, he was an excellent cook—a bottle of whiskey mysteriously appeared. Knowing these mountains and their strange effects on man, Magill had expressly forbidden alcohol, but since it was here he saw no reason to waste it. The evening acquired the aspects of a party.

"You know," Andy said, "I'm almost tempted to invite those Indians over for a drink."

"Presuming they're not on the mountain already," someone interjected.

Despite the thought, the mood was so cheerful no one thought to post a guard.

It wasn't really necessary, for Magill slept little that night. Earlier, in Apache Junction, he had himself yielded to temptation, purchasing a huge feather-down pillow. Although now ensconced in comfort—or as much as a sleeping bag on hard rock could provide—he lay awake reviewing clues.

If you passed the three red hills, the Dutchman said, you've gone too far. The three red hills were about a half-mile north of Bluff Springs Mountain. They hadn't gone too far.

In their conversation with Mason, the two soldiers had described their route from the mine area out of the mountains. Mentally backtracking the route, Magill found himself in Needle Canyon.

In his last note Adolph Ruth had referred to a "monumental trail" on which "the monument has long been destroyed." This could refer to the stone face, which the Apaches had rolled off the mountain. In the same note he had written: "Travel northward, in the gorge, and up over a lofty ridge, thence downward past the Needle into a canyon running north, and finally into a tributary canyon, very steep and rocky, and densely wooded with a continuous thicket of scrub oak." The canyon running north was obviously Needle Canyon, while the description of the tributary canyon tallied perfectly with the area of their explorations.

Thus far, everything fit.

The day began auspiciously. The two sentinels were no longer in sight. Nor, using binoculars, could they discern any trace of the six armed prospectors said by Crandall to be on Black Top.

A little more than an hour was required to reach the south end of the mountain. Once here, however, they encountered problems. From on top the terrain looked different; they explored a half-dozen ravines before, early in the afternoon, finding the one that led down to the tunnel.

The wind was strong, the terrain rugged. It was here, on these overhanging precipices, that Jim Bark had saved the life of Sims Ely when he slipped and nearly went over the side. Ely and Bark had not attempted to go down the cliffs, however, as Bark suffered from acrophobia, fear of heights.

Magill wondered how many of his companions were so

afflicted, remembering how on his first descent down the side of the mountain he had hugged the rocks. Usually the fear passed quickly, when other things caught the attention. Yet one panicked man could kill them all and this was why, after considerable thought, he decided against linking the group together with rope.

Slowly they descended, Magill in the lead. He had gone down about fifty feet when he stepped on some loose shale and stumbled forward. As his torso lunged out over the edge, so that he was looking straight down into Needle Canyon several thousand feet below, his legs smashed against a boulder and held his body in place.

The fall badly bruised his right knee and ripped his pants straight down the leg.

This time, when they started again, it was with ropes around their waists, and with Baker in the lead, Andy, Jim, and Magill following, in that order.

The slope was steep, yet not too steep for mules. Another important clue fit.

They were more than halfway down the mountain when Baker and Andy stepped onto a narrow ledge. As Jim stepped down also, Baker let out a yell. "The ground is sliding under me!"

As quickly as it started, the shifting stopped. A small circular area had caved in under their feet. Back under an overhanging ledge, almost covered by rocks, was an opening.

"We've found it!" Baker and Andy yelled in unison.

In the years since the Dutchman's death, a number of prospectors have claimed to have found his fabled lost mine. On examination, however, the various potholes and diggings have failed to correspond with Jacob Waltz's own precise description. For his mine was strangely shaped. "The mine is a round pit," he said, "shaped like a funnel with the large end up. Shelves had been made in the wall as the miners went deeper and on each shelf stood upright timbers with notches in them for the miners to use in climbing out of the pit with the sacks of ore on their backs. The pit was sloping to a point because the workers had shaped it that way."

Crawling to the opening on their hands and knees, the men looked down into the sloping funnel. It was exactly as the Dutchman had described it.

"From my mine I have to climb up to see Weaver's Needle," the Dutchman said. Once within the ravine, that blunt-shaped peak was hidden from view. Only on climbing up and out did it reappear.

"From the mouth of my mine I can look down and see people on the old military trail." The old military trail was Needle Canyon, directly below. "But they can't see my mine." It was true: from below the mine was concealed by the overhanging ledge.

"The rays of the setting sun shine in the mouth of my mine and illuminate my gold." It was 3 P.M. but there was no need to wait until sundown to see that the sun, setting in the west, would shine directly on this spot.

Every clue fit, from the Peralta map to the Dutchman's own words. Even Magill now had to admit that he was probably wrong in his interpretation of Ruth's hasty scrawl. The pit was located almost exactly two hundred feet above the tunnel.

"Veni, vidi, vici," he said aloud.

Yet he didn't feel like a conqueror. For he realized that to date he had been so intent upon finding the pit that he had given almost no thought to the problems ahead.

CHAPTER 9

What To Do with a Gold Mine?

WHAT DO YOU DO with a gold mine, once you've found it?

No plans had been made covering this eventuality. Not one of the men had ever filed a mining claim, nor knew the procedure for doing so. The mine was located in an extremely remote area; the ledge on which the pit opened was so narrow that only two men could work there at any one time. To transport even the most basic supplies to the top of the mountain had already proven fantastically expensive. And special mining equipment would be needed. For the Apache tale was true. The shaft had been filled in with rocks and dirt, the surface carefully concealed. But over the years the fill had settled to the point where the combined weight of the men had caused the ground to cave in slightly, betraying the location. The Dutchman had declared his shaft extended downward more than thirty feet. It would all have to be cleared before any actual mining could begin.

Magill was ostensibly the only one troubled by such thoughts. The rest were heady with excitement. "We've found the Lost Dutchman!" they kept repeating, almost in disbelief. "This calls for a celebration!" Jim proclaimed. Fortunately the last of the whiskey had been drunk the previous night. As it was, the backslapping and natural exuberance of the group several times threatened to carry them to the valley floor below.

To Magill fell the unenviable task of putting a damper on their enthusiasm.

There were two essential first steps. One, that the legal status of the mine be determined. If it were clear—if there were no prior claims—then their own claim would have to be filed as soon as possible. Two, that some form of financing be obtained. "That's no trouble," one of the men broke in happily. "I can mortgage my house and get a loan on my car." Others chorused agreement. But, as Magill was forced to point out, the money thus raised would meet only their most immediate needs. A work crew would have to be maintained at the site; this would mean flying in supplies and equipment every few days. And the expenditure of a sizable amount before—*if*, rather—one cent was recovered.

The helicopter pilot was due in at sunset with additional supplies. It was decided they would all be flown out that day, part of the group returning to Oklahoma City in the car and truck with the mules,* the others, including Magill and Charley, catching the first available flight from Phoenix. Although they were reluctant to leave the mine unprotected, there was no alternative. It was agreed that as soon as it could be arranged, as many as could would return to stake out their claim and begin operations. It was also agreed that complete secrecy be maintained, no word of the find being made public until their claim was filed.

* On reaching Oklahoma City, Satan and Pauline were turned out to the pasturage they so richly deserved.

Late that afternoon they flew off the top of Bluff Springs Mountain, leaving behind them a host of unsolved mysteries.

The following afternoon, Thursday, April 28, the group reassembled in Magill's office to formulate plans. Magill had already begun work on the first order of business. That morning he had obtained a copy of the Bureau of Land Management's pamphlet, *Mining Claims—Questions and Answers,* covering procedures for filing claims in natural wilderness areas. An attorney had been engaged to make a search of Arizona records to determine whether a valid prior claim existed.

All the men were exhausted—on this trip alone, Magill had lost fourteen pounds. Each had his own problems, both personal and financial. Yet, even after driving all night, Andy, Jim, and Baker were anxious to return to Arizona to begin digging. But first they had to arrange leave from their jobs. This posed no difficulty for Baker, whose employer was Magill. But this in turn created a special problem for the private detective, who, though utilizing the services of a number of full- and part-time operatives, directed the overall operation of the agency himself, to the point of personally determining the routine to be followed in each case. Occasionally, in the past, when he was away for a few days on special assignment, it had been possible to leave Baker in charge. Now it appeared that he would have to shut down the agency entirely, at least for the time being.

It was Thursday. The earliest anyone could get away would be the coming weekend. Magill, scheduled to testify Monday in a court case, had no idea when he could leave.

There remained a problem common to all—financing the operation. This they were discussing when the telephone rang.

It was a reporter for the *Oklahoma Journal.*

"Mr. Magill, I understand you've discovered the Lost Dutchman Mine. What's the story?"

In the pit of his stomach, Magill felt the beginning of an ulcer.

"Who told you that?" he asked.

A female relative of one of the men, who worked on the *Journal* as a proofreader, had leaked the news. The reporter lacked details, however, and was anxious to get the full story from Magill.

"I'll have to call you back." Magill hung up.

He told the others.

"Well," Charley ventured, "we can either confirm it or deny it. Either way we've got problems."

"There's one more possibility," Magill said. "We might be able to stall."

It was just possible the reporter might be willing to sit on the story until they were ready to release it—in return for promise of an exclusive.

Not necessarily the most desirable alternative, it was, nevertheless, under the circumstances, the only one they could think of; they agreed it was worth trying.

When the doorbell rang a few minutes later Magill guessed, correctly, who his caller was.

The reporter agreed readily to their terms. He would not break the story until Magill gave him permission to do so. In return, until that time, neither Magill nor his partners would discuss the matter with any other representative of the press.

For the time being, Magill gave him only the barest outline: of how he had obtained the set of Peralta maps from Dr. Ruth, and of how these, together with the Dutchman's own explicit directions, had led them straight to the mine.

Asked how much gold they had found, Magill replied: "I can't comment on that at this time."

"Have you found any gold?" he persisted.

"No comment."

"How rich do you expect the mine will be?"

"It's too early to say," Magill answered. "We, of course, hope it will be as rich as the Dutchman said it was, which would make it very, very rich indeed."

Where was the mine located?

"It's exactly where the Dutchman said it was," Magill replied. "It's right on the spot. He left many clues to the location and every one of them checked out."

None of the men had slept since leaving Arizona the previous day. The minute the reporter left, Magill adjourned the meeting, the question of financing still unresolved.

Once alone he placed a call to Washington, D.C.

"We've found your father's mine," he said.

"Somehow I had the feeling you would," Dr. Ruth replied. "Congratulations. Now I know it wasn't all in vain."

The telephone rang shortly after six the following morning. In his work, Magill was used to calls at all hours. This was no ordinary call, however.

"Mr. Magill? This is United Press International. Is the story in today's *Oklahoma Journal* true?"

The ulcer grew.

"What story? I haven't seen the paper yet. It's still on the front porch."

"Go get it. I'll hold on."

Magill opened the paper. There was a big, black, two-bank headline on the front page:

LOST DUTCHMAN MINE FOUND?
LOCAL DETECTIVE SAYS SO

Magill was so angry he had trouble focusing on the type. But he forced himself to sit down and read it through. The "facts" were incredibly garbled. In reply to the question concerning the gold, Magill was quoted as saying, "I believe that the mine is even richer than anyone can imagine. I believe it is many times richer than even the Dutchman ever dreamed."

Reading on, he discovered the reporter had also called Dr. Ruth and questioned him concerning the authenticity of the maps and the find. "If Mr. Magill has found the same mine I believe my father found," Dr. Ruth was quoted as saying, "then he has found the Lost Dutchman Mine."

Magill had no choice but to confirm the story. However, he did succeed in straightening out some of the errors in the account. It would prove to be a futile gesture.

The UPI call was followed almost immediately by one from AP, then others from each of the networks—CBS, NBC, and ABC. By nine o'clock all four of his extensions were ringing. On the noon news from Chicago, Magill was quoted as saying: "I have taken nuggets out of the mine as big as my fist." A still later broadcast, equally inventive, had Magill and his partners finding a cave full of skeletons, one of them presumably that of Adolph Ruth. By early afternoon Magill had lost count of the calls. They included requests for exclusive story rights from various magazines and a television network, propositions from several writers, hearty congratulations from Bob Crandall in Albuquerque, frankly skeptical queries from Arizona newspapers, and an offer, from the representative of a Phoenix insurance company, who, for no fee at all, strictly for publicity value, offered to insure the group for one million dollars against the Apache curse.

Magill couldn't help smiling when he turned down the last offer. He wondered if the insurance man would have been so eager had he known of the tennis shoes, the hooting owl, and the copperhead.

There were several offers of financing. He reported them to his partners when they met again that night. It was important, he cautioned, that each offer be carefully investigated before any decision was reached. It would be no problem for him to run a background check on the companies, although it might take a few days.

He suspected that at least one of the offers was bogus, the voice of one caller sounding suspiciously like that of an Arizona reporter who had talked with him earlier.

Most of the men didn't want to wait, however. One offer appealed to them especially. It was from a man who will here be called William Harold, a well-known financial figure in the Southwest whose speculations in oil and mining had frequently made headlines. Harold had not only called on Magill, but also had taken pains to contact each of the other partners as well.

His offer was highly attractive. He would finance their entire operation, provide a private plane to fly the men back and forth to Arizona, underwrite the cost of supplies and equipment. In addition, he would put on salary, at $1,500 per month, any of the men who wanted to work full time at the mine. This latter feature especially pleased Baker, Andy, and Jim.

In return, Harold would be made a full partner, sharing equally in the profits, if any, after his investment was repaid. Thus, instead of six partners, there would be seven, each with a one-seventh share.

The offer seemed fair—a perfect solution to their immediate problems—but Magill wanted more time to investigate and consider it. The others, however, called for a vote, and the majority voted to accept Harold's offer.

Less than forty-eight hours after the discovery, Glenn Magill had lost all but nominal control of the operation.

Although the mine had been lost for decades, probably only one man, Adolph Ruth, having seen it in the seventy-five years since Jacob Waltz's death, and although it was located in an almost inaccessible place which, before leaving the mountain, the men had been careful to disguise again so that no trace of their presence there was evident—it now seemed, once the news of the find was out, that anyone could stumble across it and file a claim.

Sunday afternoon Harold chartered a private plane to fly Andy, Baker, and Jim to Phoenix, together with a man representing Harold's interests. They would proceed into the Superstitions immediately, to begin surveying the claim and setting up markers; the others would join them at the earliest possible moment.

Magill, who, per their original contract, still retained all publicity rights to the story, remained behind, serving as spokesman for the group. Over the weekend, as news of the discovery was picked up by newspapers around the country, all semblance of family life in the Magill household disappeared, while, to all intents and purposes, the detective agency ceased operation.

There were crackpot calls by the dozens, one from a female who claimed to be the illegitimate daughter of Jacob Waltz and Julia Thomas. For a woman who would have to be in her seventies she had a remarkably young voice.

There were more offers of financial assistance, including a preliminary query from a long-established Western mining company, which expressed interest in buying them out.

There was also a warning from an attorney who stated that their claim infringed upon that of his client. This was interesting, inasmuch as they had yet to file a claim, and the only exact statement they had offered about their discovery said merely that it was in the Superstition Mountains.

Another call was even more startling. When Magill put down the receiver he had the solution to a thirty-five-year-old mystery: he knew, without doubt, who had murdered Adolph Ruth. There was little time to consider this revelation, however, and he forced himself to put it out of mind for the present. This was no crackpot call, but it would require further checking.

The greatest pressure came from the news media, particularly in Arizona.

On Saturday a representative of one of the state's leading newspapers called Magill, informing him that there was talk in the capital of convening a special session of the Arizona State Legislature to pass a resolution commemorating the men for their find. It was reported on good authority, the newsman added, that Barry Goldwater, who had financed Barry Storm's first book, was extremely pleased at news of the discovery and that it was quite possible that Senator Goldwater would be present at the special ceremony to congratulate the man personally.

The paper, of course, would be quite willing to put its not inconsiderable influence at work behind the scenes to bring all this about—in exchange for exclusive rights to the story. It would be necessary, however, that arrangements be made immediately for reporters and cameramen to visit the site, together with a number of legislators, and a select group of businessmen—say "thirty or so"—representing the Dons Club of the Phoenix Chamber of Commerce.

Magill asked for time to consider the proposition.

But he quickly put this out of mind too. They had barely begun their explorations. It was important that a careful, foot-by-foot search of the area be made. Even disregarding the mine and the tunnel, there were other mysteries yet to be solved. Where was the Dutchman's hidden cache? Waltz himself had left no clue to its location—except to say that it contained about $20,000 in gold and was somewhere near his base camp. Where was Wiser's body buried? And the bodies of the two Mexicans accidentally killed by Waltz and Wiser? Any clues that might still remain could be obliterated by a group so large. There was also the question of safety. When Magill had mentioned the ruggedness of the area, the newsman had appeared to take it almost as a challenge. The last thing they needed at this point was fifty or more men stumbling over the sheer cliffs of Bluff Springs Mountain.

This call had come on Saturday. It was repeated on Sunday. On Monday the newsman reported that Senator Goldwater was reportedly disturbed by Mr. Magill's lack of cooperation. "Of course, *I* don't feel this way, Mr. Magill—and I'm *quite sure* the senator doesn't either—but there are some very prominent people in Phoenix who feel that you have no right to the mine. They say—of course, these are their words, not mine, or the senator's—that there should be a law which prohibits an 'Okie' from coming in and stealing one of Arizona's leading tourist attractions."

Magill was also informed that one of the local papers had already labeled the whole story a monumental fraud, claiming to have proof that the Oklahoma men had never been inside the Superstitions.

Late Monday evening, with a great sense of relief, Magill and Charley left Oklahoma City for the one place they were sure had no telephone.

There was a different mood atop Bluff Springs this time. Arguments seemed to break out spontaneously, without reason. Even the simplest decisions brought disagreements. In descending the cliffs to the mine, no one wanted to go first. Each had a logical explanation. No one was fooled. Not an ounce of gold had been found, yet already the men distrusted each other.

Once, en route from base camp to the head of the ravine, Magill noticed that one of the men had dropped behind. Quietly backtracking, he found him attempting to hide one of the large canvas waterbags in a crevice in the rock. Seeing Magill, he reached quickly for his sidearm, but Magill was faster.

Holding the gun on him, Magill ordered him to unsnap and drop his holster. He did so, reluctantly. "Now toss me the bag,"

Magill ordered. He threw it to him, with a look of pure hatred.

Magill turned up the bag, took a huge swallow, then poured the remainder of its contents on the ground.

Holstering his gun but keeping one hand on the butt, Magill tossed back the empty bag. "Now pick up your gun—and stop acting like an ass."

When they went down trail this time, Magill followed.

The incident was inexplicable; the basin in the hidden valley contained more than enough water for their needs. It also marked the end of a friendship. Although both men would later attempt to patch over the incident, they would never quite succeed.

What disturbed Magill most was not the attempt to hide the bag but how close, in his anger, he had come to using the gun.

Andy and Jim had already begun clearing the pit. Despite the cramped area in which they had to work, the initial digging was relatively easy, the men simply tossing the dirt and rocks off the side of the mountain. It was already apparent, however, that the deeper they dug the more difficult it would be to transport the fill to the surface. To climb out of the pit with each shovelful would break the strongest man in hours. A bucket-and-hoist arrangement was impossible, because of the overhanging cliffs above the mine. And there was no way to bring heavy equipment into the area. Only one possibility seemed feasible—dynamite, to blast out the fill. None of the men had experience with explosives, but as Jim put it, "We're willing to experiment!"

Had the Apaches filled the pit?

Charley, ever skeptical, wondered if the fill—which consisted of dirt, rocks, and a few small boulders—might have washed down from above. Careful examination convinced him otherwise. If water had been present, the fill would have been tightly packed. It wasn't. It was loose, so loose it could be scooped out with a shovel. If a landslide was responsible, then it would have filled haphazardly. Many of the rocks were laid out in rows.

The mine was hand-filled. And the fill had been carried a considerable distance. While the walls of the shaft were of a smooth, blackish stone, the fill was of entirely different composition, mostly a reddish sandstone not native to the immediate area. After a brief search atop Bluff Springs Mountain, Magill and Charley found rocks and soil to match, in the hidden valley.

While Andy and Jim alternated in the pit, Magill and the others set up stone markers and claim notices. They also made a careful search of the area for other markers but found none. To date, through all their explorations in both the pit and tunnel areas, they had found no evidence of anyone's having been in the vicinity in recent times.

There was in America at least one place where there were no broken bottles, beer cans, or cigarette butts.

The next morning there was a whoop and holler from the pit. *"Gold!"* Jim yelled in a voice that would have rivaled that of Samuel Brannan.

Admittedly it was not much—a trace of color in a few pieces of rose quartz, similar to that Magill had found on an earlier trip—but it was important, not only because the Dutchman's gold had been in rose quartz but because, according to mining laws, unless a valuable mineral is found there can be no valid claim.

There are four simple steps for filing a claim:

(1) The actual physical exposure or "discovery" of a valuable mineral.

(2) Distinctively and clearly marking and establishing the boundaries of the claim on the ground so that it can be readily

identified. This is usually done by putting up posts or stone monuments on all four corners of the claim.

(3) Posting the notice of location on the claim in a conspicuous place, usually at the place of discovery.

(4) Recording an exact copy of the location in the appropriate office, usually the County Recorder's office in the county where the claim is located.

The men had fulfilled the first three steps. Only the fourth remained.

In putting up the markers, they had staked out not one claim but six—each a rectangle covering the maximum permissible distance of 600 × 1,500 feet. This was done to include both the pit and tunnel areas, as well as the probable course the vein would follow once it was uncovered. But it also served another function. Once the claim papers were filed, the general location —Bluff Springs Mountain—would no longer be secret. By filing six claims in the region, however, they could make it impossible for anyone else to pinpoint specifically the actual mine site.

Whether the location still remained a secret, however, was questionable. Several times during the past two days the men had seen a helicopter flying over the area. Although it never came in close, it could quite possibly spot them. Later they were told that the copter had been hired by a Phoenix television station in an unsuccessful attempt to find them. At the time, however, it seemed to represent a different threat: claim jumping. Although they were anxious to continue their explorations—particularly of the tunnel, with its mysterious "door"— when the helicopter pilot brought in supplies Wednesday evening, they flew out with him, leaving two men to guard the site.

Registering under assumed names, they spent the night at the Red Rock Motel in Mesa. During the evening Magill slipped out. Using an outside phone, he called their attorney. The news was good. The record search had failed to disclose any prior claims on the area in question.

Early the next morning, after renting a car, they began making the rounds of government offices in Phoenix. They had been warned by the attorney that occasionally a valuable claim is contested and set aside because the filers have failed to process through all the proper federal and state agencies. To forestall any such possibility, they visited every federal and state office that might conceivably have an interest in their project, including the U.S. Forest Service, the Geological Survey office, the Department of the Interior, the Bureau of Land Management, and the Bureau of Mines.

Shortly after noon, they drove to the courthouse in Florence, county seat of Pinal County, only to find that several reporters had anticipated them. Actually they had been waiting there since announcement of the find.

The County Recorder, Sophie Smith, was out to lunch. Her deputy refused to accept the filing papers. "There has never been a claim filed on the Lost Dutchman Mine before, and I have no intention of filing the first. What are you people trying to do—put us out of business?"

Magill, who had anticipated possible trouble, had been advised by the Bureau of Mines that so long as the papers were properly filled out and the filing fee paid, the County Recorder could not refuse to accept them. The function of the recorder, he had been told, was simply that of an official notary public. That office could neither contest a claim nor declare it valid or invalid. The latter question would eventually be determined by the federal government, in granting patent to the land.

Magill firmly held his ground. At 12:35 P.M. on Thursday, May 5, 1966, he and his partners filed six claims on the mine they called "The Dutchman."

It was one of the last things they did with complete unanimity. Over the next several weeks the arguments multiplied. Approached logically, in retrospect, they sounded almost nonsensical. Most often they were not over actualities but suspicions —that one of the men had found something and was keeping it from the others, that several of the men were plotting against one or more of the others. Much of this was due to failure in communications; the men on Bluff Springs Mountain were never quite sure what the men in Oklahoma City were doing, and vice versa.

And some of it was carefully fostered.

On May 16 the partners met in Oklahoma City, where they officially incorporated under the laws of the State of Oklahoma as The Lost Dutchman Exploration Company.

Harold took full charge. He not only had the proxy votes of the men at the mine, but had also bought out Carl Lee, for whom one trip into the Superstitions had been enough.

After much argument, it was finally agreed that 1,000 shares of stock would be issued to each partner. If he wanted to sell it, that would be his business but there would be no public offering. Par value was set at $1 per share.

Someone suggested that the first 1,000 shares—Certificate No. 1—be issued to Glenn D. Magill and that he be unanimously elected president of the corporation.

"Just a minute," Harold interrupted. "Mr. Magill, would you mind telling us exactly what you've done to earn a full share?"

Magill, in disgust, walked out of the room. "I've had it," he said, asking that his name be dropped from consideration.

In his absence, Magill was voted the No. 1 Certificate, and Harold was elected president, Charles Rhoades secretary.

With almost a sense of relief, Magill turned his attention to salvaging what remained of his business and family life. He again took on cases and tried to concentrate on his work.

The respite was short-lived. It was soon apparent that despite Harold's grandiose, if vague, plans for making the mine pay, most of the practical day-to-day arrangements still remained on the shoulders of Magill, Rhoades, and the others.

Although Andy and Jim spent the greater part of their time at the mine, the others flew back and forth from Oklahoma whenever they could get away. There was transportation to arrange (now, more often than not, when the men needed it, the private plane was unavailable); helicopter schedules to set up; supplies to be purchased. In coordinating activities between Oklahoma City and Phoenix, Magill's own phone bill ran to more than five hundred dollars per month. He paid it himself. As time passed, more and more of the corporation bills remained unpaid, including salary checks due the men at the mine.

Next to helicopter rental, the largest expense was dynamite. The first several attempts to use it had nearly been fatal, and it was necessary to fly in a mining expert. After examining the pit and tunnel sites, he strongly recommended that all dynamiting in the tunnel be halted, at least while work was proceeding in the pit above. Prior to this the men had tried to blast open the door in the tunnel wall, using minute quantities of explosives. The resultant explosion had leveled some trees but left the tunnel wall undented. The engineer now pointed out several rock traps above the tunnel and surrounding it, places where the touching of a single rock could send a huge boulder tumbling down.

"This place has been rigged," he said authoritatively. "It's a wonder that any of you are still around."

Who had set up the rocks this way? Jacob Waltz said that before leaving the mine for the last time he had built a rock wall covering the entrance to the tunnel. Dearing said that when he found the mine some of the rocks had fallen down, and he had torn down some of the others, to look in. But these were around and above the tunnel, not over the entrance. It seemed unlikely that Waltz would have gone to all this trouble to protect something in which he and Wiser admittedly weren't interested. His only reason for walling over the tunnel had been to hide this clue to the presence of the mine. If not Waltz, who? And, more important, why? Why all this protection of the tunnel rather than the pit?

Despite their curiosity, the men were not entirely unhappy about discontinuing operations in the tunnel. Neither Andy nor Jim was of superstitious bent, yet both felt a vague uneasiness while working here. "It's hard to explain," Andy once remarked. "It's a kind of dark feeling, as if we're not wanted."

Magill knew exactly what he meant. Of the film taken on Bluff Springs Mountain not one photo of the tunnel had developed. Charley had tried flashbulbs, time exposures, different film, and different times of the day. The result was always the same—other photos on the roll came out perfectly; negatives of the tunnel shots were entirely black.

Could it be radiation? Magill asked the clerk in the camera store. No, he replied, he'd had experience with that; in those cases the film was overexposed; this film reacted as if it hadn't ever been exposed.

The discoveries continued.

On a rock just above the tunnel, they found a weatherworn carving: a hexagon with a dot in the center; and, below that, a crawling snake.

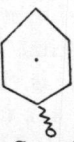

The dotted hexagon was a Spanish symbol for treasure; the snake's direction indicated its location. Had the snake been traveling upward, it would have pointed to the mine. But it pointed down, straight into the tunnel.

Some 10 feet down in the pit itself, another carving appeared on the wall. This was a wedge-shaped outline; above it was the letter "S"; to the right and toward the bottom were the letters "DON."

What did it mean?

Magill was not sure. The drawing seemed to be a crude representation of the top of Bluff Springs Mountain, the line down the center following the course of the hidden valley. If this was meant to be Bluff Springs, this could explain the "S" on the top, for as depicted this was the south end of the mountain. "Don" was a fairly common honorary title in Spanish-speaking countries. It could possibly have referred to Don Miguel Peralta; then again, in earlier times, it had been sometimes used as a church title and might have referred to a specific priest.

The drawing was devoid of any specific location or treasure or mine symbol, such as an X. And why would it be carved here?

Magill didn't know the answers.

A few feet farther down in the pit, the loose fill suddenly stopped. Their shovels clanged against something hard and unyielding. With rising excitement, they shoveled the fill aside, only to uncover what appeared to be a layer of cement. Carefully examined, it more closely resembled caliche—the crust or crusts of calcium carbonate that forms on top of stony soil in arid and semiarid regions and is especially common in Arizona. But could it be formed this far underground? After considerable blasting, the men succeeded in breaking off some samples, which Magill showed to a geologist at the University of Oklahoma. It wasn't caliche, he said, or any kind of modern cement. Checking further, Magill learned that the Indians of the Southwest had once mixed their own form of cement. The exact formula was now lost in time, but one of its ingredients was known to have been animal blood. Mixed and exposed to air, it quickly dried, leaving a hard, extremely tough surface. Could this be the same substance? The geologist didn't know, but thought it possible. If it was the same, when the Indians said they had sealed up the mine, they must have meant it literally.

All this was secondary, however, to a far more important question. How thick was the seal? There was only one way to tell. Larger quantities of explosives would have to be brought in, in an attempt to blast through.

The most puzzling find, however, was four stone guardhouses or lookouts that had been built into the side of Bluff Springs Mountain, surrounding the tunnel at some distance.

Identical in construction, each large enough to hold two men, these had been cut straight into the rock and then, stone by stone, carefully walled up by hand, leaving only a small space for entry and exit. From these lookouts the whole valley floor could be seen. Yet unless one were directly upon them—Charley and Baker had found the first one accidentally while attempting to descend the cliffs on a rope—they were invisible, so perfectly did they match the surrounding terrain.

Jacob Waltz had never mentioned them. It was possible that in his single-minded attention to the mine he never saw them. Yet, they were obviously ancient in construction—easily ancient enough to predate Waltz.

Who built them? There were not a great many possibilities, for until modern times the Superstitions had known only a few peoples: the Indians, the Spanish, and the Mexicans. If the Indians built them, what were they defending? Certainly not a gold mine, for to them gold meant nothing. Then too, there was the matter of their location. They surrounded the tunnel, not the mine. Again, why?

All that was certain was that someone had felt that something in this area warranted protection, even if it involved the expenditure of a great amount of time and effort.

More and more evidence was accumulating to indicate that the tunnel was far more than the blind alley it had first seemed.

None of the pressure on Magill had eased; it had simply assumed different forms.

Following the filing of the claim papers, Magill had received letters from several attorneys, each representing a different client, each claiming that Magill and his partners were trespassing on their client's claim. No actual suits were filed, however, and the letters all had one phrase in common. Magill and his partners were given a choice of vacating the claim immediately or of meeting with the attorney and his client "to attempt to reach an amicable settlement."

In the words of the immortal Durante, "Everybody wants to get into the act."

These were, at the moment, the least of Magill's worries.

On Sunday, May 1, three days after the discovery story broke, Station KTVK, Channel 3, in Phoenix, had carried an extraordinary announcement on its evening news program.

"For the first time in history," the newscaster reported, "the Apache Indians are going to tell their story of the Sacred Mountains which the white men call the Superstitions."

According to Philip Cassadore, spokesman for the Apache medicine men, "there have been many events and news items which have been part of the reason for the decision for the Apaches to reveal some of their religion and history pertaining to the Sacred Mountains."

These revelations were to be made at a special pow-wow, to be called the following week.

The broadcast concluded, "The Apache believes that the Sacred Mountains are the home of the Mountain Spirits. The

Mountain Spirits are a secret society who do a special work. When an Apache dies his soul must pass through the Sacred Mountains and it is the Mountain Spirits' work to lead him either to heaven or to hell as his final abode."

Despite the buildup, when the pow-wow finally convened, the promised revelations were not made.

At the time Magill, who had been kept posted on these developments by Shirley Clum, of KTVK, had wondered about the odd silence. But then, in the press of other matters, he had forgotten it. Events now recalled it to mind.

Although weeks had passed since the men at the mine had last seen the solitary watchers on Black Top, they now found more tennis-shoe tracks. Only this time they were not in Needle Canyon but on the top of Bluff Springs Mountain. Late one afternoon, as they were climbing from the pit to the summit, a shower of rocks came down, narrowly missing Andy and Jim. From their position they could see no one, yet they heard a sound like running feet. Occasionally at night several of the other men, including Magill, had heard what they thought were footsteps. These could have been made by animals, but, to date, they had seen none atop the mountain.

It might be that all these incidents, as well as those transpiring before, were coincidental and bore no relation to the Indians. (Some old-timers in the area, including Morrow, say that they have never seen an Indian in the Superstitions; there are also others, perhaps best left unnamed, although their letters have appeared in *True West* and *Frontier Times,* who claim to have seen hundreds, all pygmies.) If only to set nerves at rest, Magill decided it was time to make peace with the Apaches.

In the past Glenn Magill & Associates had represented a number of Indian clients in the Southwest. One, an Apache from Oklahoma City, was especially active in intertribal affairs. Magill had attempted to discuss the Superstitions with him on one previous occasion, while still in the preliminary stage of his Lost Dutchman search. However, given evasive replies to his questions, he had not pursued the matter further.

He called on him now to request a special favor.

The chief governing body of the reservation Apaches is the Apache Tribal Council. Magill asked if he would be willing to take a message to them.

Over his long investigation, Magill said, he had developed a respect for both the Apache people and their sacred mountains.

The Indian nodded; he knew that.

Often in his search, Magill continued, he had heard it said that somewhere in these mountains there was an area especially holy to his people.

The Indian's face remained impassive.

If he and his partners had trespassed on this area, they had done so unknowingly, Magill said. If they had in any way offended the Apache people by breaking one of their taboos, they wished to be informed of this fact, that it might not be repeated. They had no wish, he said, to defile holy ground or to show disrespect for any of the Apache beliefs or customs.

The message was duly delivered. In reply Magill was thanked for his expression of concern. For a time he heard nothing more.

One day in June, while Andy was in Apache Junction buying additional supplies, there was a knock on his motel door. His visitor, a tall, handsome Apache, identified himself as John Surackus, representative of the San Carlos Reservation.

"I came to tell you that you have been working on our sacred ground."

It was less a warning than a simple statement of fact, delivered with a complete lack of emphasis or emotion.

"Are there graves there or something?" Andy asked. "A burial ground?"

Surackus didn't reply.

"Just where is this area, so we can avoid it?"

In answer, Surackus repeated his message, in identical words, turned, and left.

"Just where have you been working, other than at the mine?" Magill asked Andy, when told of this development.

The day prior to the visit, Andy said, he and Baker and Jim had done some digging under the stone face in Needle Canyon. Baker had gotten the idea that there might be something buried under the huge monolith, but they had spent only a short time there and had found nothing.

It was agreed that further digging in this area be discontinued.

The men never heard from Surackus again. Neither did they see any more tennis-shoe tracks.

There was no tangible proof, nothing except a changed feeling, and it may have been entirely a product of the men's imaginations, but from this time forth the crew on Bluff Springs believed that the Apaches were watching over them protectively.

There would be more incidents—the worst yet to come—but from this point they looked elsewhere for explanations.

Making peace with the whites proved more difficult, but equally essential.

As Magill and his partners continued to refuse to allow visitors to the site, several Arizona papers began hinting, none too subtly, that the whole discovery was a fake. With remarkable patience, Magill refused to be baited, even when one trod far into the domain of libel. Yet he was disturbed by the growing hostility as evidenced in some of the rumors being circulated.

As with many of their activities, their large dynamite purchases had not gone unnoticed. It was now charged that in their greedy lust for gold they were wantonly destroying important natural and historical landmarks.

Magill's chief gossip source, the Arizona reporter, informed him of still another rumor. Rather than memorializing their find, there was now talk of introducing a special law in the legislature to prohibit out-of-state residents from removing gold from the state.

Although the question was largely rhetorical—no quantity of gold worth removing having yet been found—on hearing the same tale from several different people, Magill consulted their attorney.

The threat was meaningless, the attorney said. This was federal land, over which the state had no jurisdiction.

Still, the talk bothered Magill, particularly the dynamite charge. Arizonans have a fierce pride in the history of their state, and rightly so. Obviously some effort would have to be made to prove the rumors baseless.

Since the story had first broken, one of Magill's most persistent callers had been George Scott, of radio station KCUB in Tucson, a CBS affiliate. Unlike the reporter who felt called upon to inform Magill of every bit of Arizona gossip, apparently in the hope of frightening him into parting with his story, Scott had been unfailingly polite and sympathetic to their problems. Moreover, he had never betrayed any of Magill's confidences.

Scott, too, wanted something—to deliver the first live radio broadcast from the site of the Lost Dutchman Mine.

He now proposed a solution to both their problems. With Magill's permission, he contacted Sidney Brinkerhoff, of the Arizona Pioneers' Historical Society in Tucson. Brinkerhoff, a respected authority on Southwestern history, had made a special study of the legends and lore of the region, including the lost mine stories, of which the Lost Dutchman Mine was the granddaddy of all.

Scott proposed that Brinkerhoff visit the site and report his findings over the air. Brinkerhoff was willing, but imposed a single condition: that he be allowed to "call it as he saw it." And, as he honestly admitted to Scott, although he promised to consider their claim with as open a mind as possible, he was, like a great many other Arizonans, frankly skeptical. Over the years the Dutchman had been "found" at least a dozen times.

Magill readily agreed. He imposed only one condition of his own: that the exact location not be mentioned on the broadcast, so that they wouldn't be overrun with sightseers while still dynamiting.

Scott arranged a network hookup. By way of prelude, each day for two weeks prior to the broadcast KCUB carried special five-minute spot announcements, during which Brinkerhoff related the history of the Superstitions, from the ancient Indian era through the period of the Mexican miners and the Dutchman to the deaths of Adolph Ruth and James Cravey.

For the broadcast itself, which drew one of the largest listening ratings in the history of Arizona radio, the KCUB crew packed into the Superstitions on mules, then—with the Forest Service looking the other way—were lifted by helicopter from Needle Canyon to the summit of Bluff Springs.

For several hours preceding the broadcast, Brinkerhoff looked, listened, and asked questions. As for his own conclusions, he kept them to himself. Carefully, he examined the pit (the men had now blasted most of the way through the seal), the various carvings, the tunnel, and the walled-in lookout posts (these, he did venture, could be Mexican or Spanish).

It was to be a most realistic broadcast. Even the most casual listener could tell that the announcer was frightened to death.

"There is," Brinkerhoff began, "a great deal more here than I thought in the first place."

Point by point he reviewed the Lost Dutchman Mine legend. And point by point, he noted, it matched the find.

In conclusion he said, "Many people have searched for the

Lost Dutchman gold mine. Certainly of the hundreds of people who have gone into the Superstitions seeking fortune and success the group from Oklahoma City, the Lost Dutchman Exploration Company, it would appear, has come closer to matching their location and their claim with the story and legend of the Peralta-Lost Dutchman mine. In fact, through many years of painstaking research, aerial photographs, and the use of a map reputed to belong to Mr. Ruth, who was killed in the nearby mountains, these gentlemen have pieced together a very likely story. In looking at the mine it is safe to say that their mine certainly matches more closely more aspects of the legend than any before recorded. If this is so, it must mean of course that the legend has some truth in it. . . .

"The significance of this discovery is in a close parallel with descriptions of the mine left to us in years past. If in the weeks ahead, they are to hit pay dirt, it will be because they have gone at this project with a conscientious and scientific approach. Certainly they've put a lot of hard work into the project. And in the end they probably will come closer to the truth than any group in the past."

It was a qualified statement, but stronger than Magill had hoped for. Most important, Brinkerhoff also made it clear that the men were not blindly destroying historical landmarks, but making every possible effort to preserve any finds.

The pressure from Arizona immediately subsided.

There were other problems, however, closer to home.

The first call was from the helicopter pilot: one of Harold's checks had bounced.

For the first several weeks Harold had paid the men at the mine regularly, as promised. Then the checks stopped. When pressed for payment of these and other outstanding bills that had accumulated, Harold had finally written more checks. A number of these now bounced.

Magill was ready to bring the men back from the mine when Harold called to ask that Magill and Charley meet him that afternoon. Rhoades, as secretary, was requested to bring along the books of the corporation.

Magill demanded an accounting. Harold refused to give it. Considering the circumstances, Harold seemed unusually smug. Exactly what he had in mind will probably never be known, for while Magill was still arguing with him, Charley was counting the number of men in the room. Quietly he picked up the books, went outside to his car, and drove home.

Without Charley, there was not a quorum present, and the meeting could not be called to order.

Harold stormed out in a rage.

More of Harold's checks bounced, including several passed in Apache Junction, a fact the local paper was quick to pick up.

Had they known what Magill knew, their headlines would have been bolder.

About this time two FBI men called on Magill and questioned him regarding sale of stock in the corporation. Magill assured them that there had been no public offering, that the stock was privately subscribed and was not available on the market. Only then did he learn that for some weeks a group of swindlers had been operating in the Phoenix area, selling thousands of shares of stock in the mine, using the name of Magill, his partners, and their corporation.

Fortunately, when the culprits were caught some time later, the papers made it clear that the actual company was in no way involved. But the taint of suspicion remained. Over the coming weeks the subject would pop up again and again, whenever the men tried to obtain vital financing.

Magill got a message to the men at the mine, via the helicopter pilot, asking them to return to Oklahoma City immediately.

The meeting was heated.

Harold defended himself by saying that he had postdated the checks, that if they had held on to them a little longer they would have cleared without trouble.

Angrily, Jim shook his check under Harold's nose. It was not postdated but long overdue.

In reply, Harold made his most serious mistake to date. He charged that the men had not really earned their salaries.

Almost all of the physical labor at the mine had been done by two men: Andy and Jim. Both had given up their jobs and left their families for weeks at a time, to work long hours under impossibly difficult and harrowing conditions, including what they were sure were several attempts on their lives.

Through Harold's harangue, Andy said nothing. When he finished, Andy quietly lifted his massive frame from the chair in which he had been sitting and swung once.

There was a dull crunch as Harold's nose caved in.

A few minutes later a vote was called and Glenn D. Magill was unanimously elected president of the Lost Dutchman Exploration Company.

CHAPTER 10

The Vanishing Pit

THE INCIDENTS continued.
On their return to Needle Canyon an angry Al Morrow accused Andy and Jim of attempting to murder him.

Two days earlier, in coming around the base of Bluff Springs Mountain, he had heard a sharp "ping" on the rocks beside him. Dropping to the ground and crawling behind a boulder, he lay there for several hours in the broiling sun, before summoning enough courage to crawl away and return to his camp.

"Why do you think *we* did it?" Jim asked.

"Because the report of the shot came from right up there." He pointed to the tunnel area.

"Two days ago we were in Oklahoma City," Andy explained. "We just got back."

"Then who shot at me?" Morrow asked.

They had to admit they didn't know.

Later, talking it over, they realized that had Morrow been killed by the shot, they would have been the logical suspects.

It was now mid-June. Daily the temperature passed 100 degrees. Huge sun blisters appeared on the skin, popped, then blistered again. There was no shelter atop Bluff Springs, except a crude lean-to constructed by the men. They found it impossible to work more than a few hours each day. As a result, progress in the pit was almost negligible. For a time they even lost ground, as the dynamite, loosening the rocks above, was sifting more dirt into the pit than they could excavate. To remedy this, they had to blast away the ledges and widen the flat area behind the pit. And this took still more time.

One day Andy hiked out for supplies. In order to lose no more of the few cool hours than necessary, when arranging his return he asked the pilot to stay at the motel overnight, leaving his copter on the flat behind the parking lot.

They arose as false dawn purpled the Superstitions, Andy carrying out supplies while the pilot made his preflight check. What he discovered nearly ended the helicopter trips.

Beaming the flashlight under the plane, he spotted something odd. At first he thought it was just a shadow, a trick of the light, and continued with his check. But his curiosity was aroused; crawling underneath on his hands and knees, he saw that a piece of rope had been secured to the fuselage. The other end of the rope seemed to disappear into the ground. He gave it a yank. The dirt fell off, revealing that it led away from the plane. He followed it for a hundred feet, to where it was securely tied to the base of a telephone pole.

Had he overlooked the foot or so of telltale hemp, the helicopter would have risen up in the air for 100 feet, jerked once, then come straight down.

There was no clue as to who had tried to kill them. But it was obvious that both Andy and Jim were being watched. On their trips out the men used different motels, different names. On three separate occasions after this they found notes under their doors. The wording varied but the handwriting was the same, as was the gist of the message. Stay out of the Superstitions or die.

It was only after considerable pleading and a rate increase to ninety dollars per hour that the pilot was persuaded to continue the trips. Even at that he was reluctant, and in early July, when called for a flight, he said he couldn't make it due to an extended government contract. From this time on, the men had to hike in and out. This not only cost them a day coming and going, since they could carry only a limited amount of supplies per man, but also greatly reduced the time they could remain at the site.

On the return from one trip out they discovered that during their absence someone had peppered the camp area with rifle fire, riddling their water tanks. The spring in Needle Canyon now being dry, they were left dependent upon the pools in the hidden valley, which were very low.

Early in August, Magill received a long-distance call from Phoenix. Jim and Andy were in the hospital, poisoned.

There was a logical explanation. As the water holes began drying up, the minerals in the water became highly concentrated, to the point of toxicity. Having spent more time at the site than anyone else, the pair had consumed large quantities of the water. The result, acute kidney poisoning.

This, at least, was the most logical explanation.

Since none of the other partners was able to get away, more than a month passed before work at the mine was resumed. This was all the more frustrating since, after several months of hard, uninspiring labor, the search had again grown exciting.

After breaking through a second seal, about twenty-five feet down, the nature of the fill had changed. It now consisted almost entirely of mine tailings.

By this time there was little left of the "partnership."

Carl Lee had been the first to drop out, selling his shares to Harold. Harold had then gone "inactive," the other men picking up and making good his bad checks. During the summer Baker Looney also dropped out, selling his shares to Jim. He had quit working for Glenn D. Magill & Associates sometime earlier. By fall of 1966 Jim and Andy were no longer speaking to Magill, and vice versa. The reasons were sometimes absurd, often petty, but cumulative. Underneath the various complaints, Magill was disappointed with the lack of progress at the mine, while Andy and Jim felt that their work wasn't being adequately appreciated. Only Charley was on speaking terms with both groups, playing the difficult role of middleman.

It was from Charley that Magill got most of the news from Bluff Springs, good and bad.

The latter predominated.

Finally unable to hold back their curiosity, Andy and Jim had dynamited the "door" in the tunnel wall. When the smoke and dust cleared they climbed up into the tunnel to pick up the riches. They were evenly split as to whether they'd find Geronimo's gold or the Jesuit cache.

There was only a gaping cavity. The door had in reality been nothing more than stone that had taken on this rectangular shape. Behind it was only a natural hole. It concealed nothing.

For a time the developments in the pit more than compensated for the disappointment. At about forty feet, when, according to the Dutchman, they should be reaching the end of the shaft and coming onto the vein, the men heard a hollow sound. The ground under their feet felt spongy. When they pushed down on their crowbars, the dirt sifted down. Shoveling away the dirt they found a wooden floor, composed entirely of rotting iron-wood logs.

This cleared up one mystery.

In relating how they had filled in the pit, one old Apache squaw had described how they had climbed in and out of the shaft with ropes. This made no sense, since the Dutchman had said there were notched timbers in the mine, which the Peraltas had used for ladders. These timbers were placed on shelves or ledges, that circled the shaft all the way to the bottom.

When the men first began excavating the mine they had found no trace of the timbers. The shelves were there all right, but, aside from some splinters in the mine tailings, there had been no wood.

It was here now, rows of it. And with this discovery they were able to reconstruct what had happened.

In filling the mine, the Apaches had first taken down the timbers, stacking them across the bottom of the shaft. They had then dumped in all the telltale mine tailings from the area adjacent to the pit, stamping them down tight and covering them over with a layer of their durable cement. Rather than remove more dirt and rocks from the area, which in itself would have served to call attention to the site, they had then carried fill from the hidden valley across the top of the mountain and down the ravine. A second seal had been laid while this was in progress. Once the pit was filled to the top, the surface was carefully disguised so that it matched the surrounding terrain.

They had now reached the bottom of the shaft. If all clues were correct, under the timbers should be the vein.

Charley brought the news to Magill.

Andy and Jim were back in Oklahoma City. They had stopped work at the mine.

"What happened?" Magill asked, though he sensed the answer even before Charley provided it.

G

"They found the vein all right—or rather where it used to be. There's no gold, Glenn. It's all played out."

From the beginning the possibility had existed that the Lost Dutchman Mine was nothing more than a pocket mine, a fluke of nature, rich but limited. The Peraltas had started a tunnel below the mine, hoping to intercept the vein, but had left it uncompleted. Why? Possibly because there was no vein to find. Jacob Waltz had stopped working the mine at least seven years before his death. When he promised to take Julia Thomas and Reiney Petrasch there he had always talked of recovering the gold from his cache, never of working the mine itself.

Yet, though the possibility had been ever present, the men had chosen to ignore it.

Now, though by this time not even Andy and Jim were speaking, the men once again acted with a certain unanimity.

Each refused to believe this was the Lost Dutchman Mine.

Magill had doubted it longer than the others. Even though the clues had seemed to fit, there was one exception. As time passed, it had grown in importance.

This was the distance between the tunnel and the pit. Exactly how far apart were they? The question still bothered him. The others had automatically assumed the distance to be two hundred feet. Yet if the first map (*Map A*) was scale, if it was meant to be an accurate depiction, then the pit was not toward the end of the mountain where they had been digging but much higher up on the cliffs on the west side.

One clue on the map might indicate just how far. On the slope of the mountain, between the tunnel and the pit, the artist had shown three distinct stair steps, one very steep, the other two more gradual. The outline of Bluff Springs Mountain took on a similar shape. (*See Photo #1.*) It was just below this third stair step that the word *hoya,* or pit, appeared.

Suddenly curious, Magill took out the locator map (*see the upper portion of Map C*). At the top of this map was what appeared to be a ravine, with four prongs on the end. He had studied this for hours and had never been able to place it. Now he knew exactly what it was. It was the hidden valley, which branched off into four waterfall tributaries.

This map had not one but *two* X's. The smaller one, which appeared above the tunnel marking, corresponded perfectly with the empty shaft! And the larger one, the one beside which the word *Mine* appeared? It too was located on the high cliffs, just where *hoya* had appeared on the first map!

All his excitement returned. Both maps appeared to put the mine in exactly the same place.

To date, he had spent little time exploring that particular area. He resolved to remedy this.

Rather than disillusion the searchers, the empty mine had almost the opposite effect. By the last weeks of 1966, Andy and Jim had each made several trips into the Superstitions, following their own hunches. In terms of discovery, they were unsuccessful (though Jim did think, for a time, that he might have found a deposit of tungsten, which, on analysis, wasn't), but none of the men could shake the feeling that the next time might be it.

Magill left for Arizona on Christmas Day. This time, except for Charley, he had a new crew. It consisted of his brother-in-law, Herman "Shorty" Guidry, a squat, sturdily built Louisiana Frenchman, with the strength of a construction worker, which he was, and the infectious humor of an imp; and Bill Young, Magill's new assistant in the agency, who had been fascinated with the Dutchman tale most of his twenty-three years and who had made one previous trip into the Superstitions on his own.

One matter was agreed in advance; if nothing was found, this would be the last trip.

Earlier, at the north end of Bluff Springs, Charley had spotted what he thought might be a shortcut to the top of the mountain. Inhumanly steep, it had another bad point as well. At the very top it was necessary to shinny through a hole between two rocks. There were no footholds; the drop was straight down. But with some effort the group made it.

("There's a trick on the trail," Joe Dearing said; "not much of a trick—but you have to go through a hole.")

The new route took them into the hidden valley, only a short distance from their camp, cutting their climbing time to three hours. As if to compensate, snow began to fall.

"This is a heck of a time to go investigating along those cliffs," Charley said.

"There are a couple of hours of daylight left,". Magill ventured hopefully. "Is anyone else game?"

There were several sets of ledges at different levels, many wide enough for only a single man. One by one these were explored. Several reached only a short distance, then dropped off into space. On one, which appeared to extend some distance along the side of the mountain, a huge boulder, tall as a man, barred their way.

" 'From my mine I have to climb up to see Weaver's Needle,' " Magill said jokingly.

Some thick shrubbery protruded alongside the boulder; using one of the branches as a step, Charley climbed over first, followed by Magill, Shorty, and Bill. About one hundred feet farther on, the ledge petered out and they started back. This time, when Magill climbed down off the boulder, the rocks beneath his feet started to shift. Grabbing the clump of brush for support, he looked down to see a circular, funnel-shaped indentation, filled with large smoky-gray, ghostlike boulders.

"Let's get out of here," he yelled. "This place isn't safe."

As he spoke the wind suddenly rose, the snow hit them with

gale force. From somewhere across canyon, clear and distinct, came a mournful howling, starting low, then rising in volume. When they had edged their way back along the ledge, away from the area, it suddenly stopped, as did the snow and wind.

"What in the hell was that?" Shorty wondered aloud.

"What did it sound like to you?" Magill asked.

"Wolves," Shorty replied.

"Maybe coyotes," Bill ventured. "I don't think there are any wolves in the Superstitions."

"Whatever it was," Charley said, "I've never heard anything like it before. And I hope I never do again."

Back at the campsite, they built a fire to ward off the chill.

"There's something odd about that place," Charley said. "I can't explain it. But I certainly felt it."

"*Wait a minute!*" Magill slammed his forehead with the butt of his hand. "That ground that caved in! You know what we've done? We found a pit, and we walked right over it!"

"Where?" Charley said. "I didn't see any pit."

"What about you, Bill?" Magill asked, suddenly wondering if he had imagined it.

"I'm afraid I——"

"Well, I saw it," Shorty interrupted. "It was just this side of that huge boulder."

"Let's go back." Magill stood up and strapped on his canteen and gun belt.

This time, however, they had trouble locating the particular ledge. Magill thought he recognized it; after following it for some way, they found a huge boulder blocking the path that looked familiar. But there was no sign of a pit. The ground was solid rock.

Almost instantly the wind rose, the snow hit, and the howling recommenced.

"Had enough?" someone asked.

Magill hadn't, but the others had.

Before they reached camp, the blizzard had again died down to a light snow flurry and the howling ceased.

That night they discussed the "vanishing pit" in great detail. Magill was more shaken by it than by anything that had happened to him in the Superstitions. Had it been his imagination? The pit had been as real to him as were the rocks around their camp. An hallucination? If so, Shorty shared it. When questioned, he described the indentation and the wraithlike rocks perfectly. Could it have been—he did not really believe in such things, yet he had to wonder—some kind of psychic phenomenon? Charley, the authority on such matters, refused to venture a guess.

There could be only one logical explanation. In going back, they had picked the wrong ledge. Magill was determined to rise early the following morning and search until they found it, if for no other reason than to prove to himself that he had seen it.

On this, as on previous trips, the men slept under a wide ledge that sheltered them on three sides and looked out over Needle Canyon. When Magill awoke the sky was still dark. He was about to turn over and go back to sleep when he looked at his watch.

"Hey," he yelled. "It's eight o'clock and there's no sun!"

"That's impossible," Shorty mumbled. "Go back to sleep."

But it was true. The storm had assumed blizzard proportions. It was impossible to see more than a few feet.

There was only one thing to do, get out of the mountains before they froze to death. Leaving behind everything but canteens, they made the descent, only this time unable to see where they were putting their feet. To complicate things, Charley was violently ill. In Needle Canyon they lost the trail altogether, finally stumbling onto a side trail that took them miles out of their way. It took fourteen hours to reach their car at First Water.

This, they agreed, was positively the last trip.

They returned in February, 1967.

Just prior to leaving Oklahoma City, Magill resigned as president of the Lost Dutchman Exploration Company. For some time he had been concerned that some of the men were selling their stock.*

This time the weather was perfect and there was ample water in the pools in the hidden canyon. But this time they couldn't even find the ledge with the boulder. After several days they gave up in disgust.

"Since this is our last trip," Magill said when they trekked out, "I want to satisfy my curiosity about one thing. Let's do something different."

Previously, he had paid little attention to the second map, that which showed the Peralta's route from Mexico. Recently, however, he had given it considerable study and had noticed something overlooked earlier. This map also showed a *mino*, or mine. Only, as well as Magill could interpret the map, this mine seemed to be located not in the Superstitions but outside them.

"I thought you said we were going to do something different," Shorty observed dryly on being told what they were looking for.

They drove to Casa Grande, which Magill had wanted to see since reading about Kino, then swung back to Florence.

---

* Four months later, on June 7, 1967, the Oklahoma Securities Commission issued a Cease and Desist Order against the Lost Dutchman Exploration Company and all its officers, forbidding them to sell any shares of stock not first registered with the Commission as required by law, a step that had been neglected in setting up the corporation.

Magill had sold none of his stock, however. Of his 1,000 shares he still owned 999, minus one share given to the author.

The lettering on this map (*see Map B*) had apparently been added by Adolph Ruth. Along the top was a river designated "Río cellim y mu prieta." Half Latin, half Spanish, this translated "River of the salt and very dark"—a perfect description of the Salt River. Along the bottom was another river, unnamed, which flowed between "Dos Buttes."

In Florence Magill obtained a topographical map. On it was a pair of mountains called Twin Buttes. And a river flowed right between them—the Gila, the old boundary between Mexico and the United States!

Now he knew they were on the right track.

Stopping at a filling station, he inquired if there was a road going north past Twin Buttes. Not exactly what you'd call a real road, the attendant told him, but there was an old river trail that just might, then again, just might not, be passable.

It was, barely. For several bumpy miles they followed it north through a long canyon, before reaching a fork. They took the road to the right. But a mile or so farther it came to a sudden dead end at a high wire fence. Up ahead was a shack. And on the hillside above it, a mine shaft.

As they started to climb out of the car, a dog came around the side of the shack, barking viciously. They climbed back in. The dog was followed by an old man and a youth, both carrying shotguns.

"What do you think you're doing?" the man asked.

"We're looking for a gold mine," Shorty said with his usual candor.

"Well, you've found it. Only we found it first. You're just about a year too late. So move on."

Backtracking, they took the other fork in the road.

"Are you thinking what I am, Bill?" Magill asked.

"That this is a part of the lode?" Bill asked.

"Right. Now let's go find our mine."

They followed the canyon for several more miles, until it too came to an abrupt end, only this time at the intersection with Highway 60. They could go no farther.

It wasn't necessary. For just beyond the highway was Queen Creek. And just beyond that, the Superstition Mountains.

Magill couldn't help laughing. "Look at this map, Bill, and tell me where our mine is."

Bill studied it for a moment. The Peraltas had crossed the Gila, traveled north past the Twin Buttes, and followed the same canyon they had been following all the way to Aroya Grande, which was Queen Creek.

"Then they went up a canyon past a 'pinicle' or peak——"

"Which is?"

"Weaver's Needle. And then, where the boxed N is, they turned north and——"

"Don't tell me," Shorty butted in. "Our mine is on Bluff Springs Mountain."

Despite his resolve, Magill could not get the vanishing pit out of his mind. Everything in his background and experience told him that things simply do not disappear.

In late April of 1967, one year after announcement of the discovery, Magill formed a new expedition. Charley was unable to get away but Bill and Shorty were still enthusiastic, and the author made up the fourth member of the party.

This time Magill was determined to set the vanishing pit to rest once and for all. Between trips he had compared notes with the other men; they had agreed on several points.

On going down the ledges for the first time, they had stopped briefly under an overhanging cliff to rest, and while lying there, Charley had done some idle digging. To the best of their recollections, this spot was on the ledge above that on which they had found the boulder.

Atop the mountain, almost directly above the pit area but just a little bit farther to the south, they had noticed a large balanced rock.

If they could find these two points, there should be no trouble locating the right spot.

Hiking in from First Water, they found the Superstitions spectacularly beautiful, the cactus in full flower. It seemed a good omen. There were others, equally auspicious, until, on reaching Needle Canyon, they found the water hole dry.

They hadn't counted on it drying up this early, so on the way in had used their water liberally, even brewing a pot of coffee.

"If there's no water in the hidden valley then we've had it," Magill observed. "We'll have to hike right back out."

On top, they found the first three pools badly polluted. There were water bugs on the fourth, however, indicating it was still pure.

While the others set up camp and started cooking supper, Bill took a hike. He returned just before dark. He had found both the ledge and the balanced rock.

"See, this is going to be a lucky trip after all," Shorty said.

One of the others proved it by making still another find—a pint of Hartley's brandy that had somehow managed to find its way into his pack.

Early the next morning the search began. Bill relocated both landmarks, and there was general agreement as to the ledge. But just to be sure, all those above it were again searched. Whether Magill was being thorough or simply avoiding the moment of confrontation, he didn't say.

The boulder was exactly where they had seen it the first time. The dense shrubbery Magill had grabbed to pull himself up, as well as the branch Shorty had used as a stair step, grew right alongside it.

But there was no pit; there was only solid rock.

Magill was not willing to give up. For two days they searched the west face of the mountain, traversing ledges so narrow they had been avoided earlier. But the results were always the same.

As a side trip, they went down mountain to the first pit. Only now it too had vanished under an avalanche of dirt and rock. Someone had set off their explosive stores—fourteen cases of dynamite, containing fifty sticks each, of 40 percent strength. Where the pit once had been, there was only rubble.

Who did it? They didn't know. And Magill frankly didn't care. The sight made him so sick he could not bring himself to go all the way down to the pit area. Totaling their expenses to date, they had wasted nearly $20,000 on this empty shaft.

Later they did learn when it happened. In March there had been a tremendous explosion of unknown origin that had cracked windows as far away as Apache Junction.

Though the cactus was still in full bloom, the trip ended far less auspiciously than it had begun. Coming down off Bluff Springs, Bill found a new trail, almost straight down, which saved them one and a half hours and added to their ages no more than thirty years. By the time they trekked out it seemed that, barring fatalities, everything possible had happened to them. The gamut ran from cactus poisoning to sunburn, from constipation to diarrhea. Magill's knee was bothering him so badly he could barely bend it. A leader had broken in one of Shorty's toes, causing it to press downward, precipitating intense and unrelieved pain. As if this weren't enough, he twisted the ankle on his other foot. His sense of humor was unaffected, however; indeed, only his jokes kept them going. As he was coming down off Black Top, where he had gone on an exploratory trip, one of Bill's legs gave out and he had to be helped along.

About two miles from First Water they collapsed beside the

trail to rest their pack sores. Someone asked the inevitable question, "Is this going to be your last trip?"

Earlier, on the mountain, each man had left something behind, from an extra pair of pants to bedrolls, ostensibly because he didn't want to carry out any unnecessary weight.

When the question was asked this time no one answered, for the simple reason that the Superstitions might hear and do their worst, knowing that this would be their last chance.

As they lay there, too tired to speak, two figures appeared over the rise of the hill. It seemed unlikely but as the pair drew closer, it was obvious that one was a woman. Clad in shorts, brown with the sun, and seemingly bursting with energy, the couple contrasted oddly with the motley-looking crew who had neither washed nor shaven for several days.

The pair stopped to pass the time, but didn't sit down as they weren't really tired. They had set out from Peralta 1 Camp a few hours before, the man said, intending to hike across the Superstitions to First Water, where a friend was to meet them in their car. They had been told to allow at least six hours for the hike. But from their progress thus far it looked as though they would make it in less than four.

He had hiked two-hundred miles already this year, the man told them proudly, and his wife had hiked more than three hundred. Just last weekend they had walked down to the bottom of the Grand Canyon—and back up.

As Magill and his crew lay exhausted by the side of the trail, the couple disappeared from view over the next ridge, moving along like two hale and hearty racehorses. They were easily in their seventies.

The Superstitions had had the last laugh.

For the time being.

Epilogue

THIS STORY is true. What makes it incredible is not that it happened but that it happened in our own time.

To some it is probably inconceivable that there exists today in the United States a place—only a few miles from civilization—where men still go so mad with the lust for gold that they turn on and kill other men they merely suspect have found it; a spot so rugged that there is little protection from the law and where, in order to adapt, man is forced to revive from his almost forgotten past his basic instincts for survival.

That the Superstitions remain such a place bothers some. It has several times been suggested that these mountains be made a national park, with wide highways for automobiles, picnic tables and camping facilities, snack bars and restaurants, maybe even a couple of motels. To date Arizonans, joined by conservationists across the country, have succeeded in fighting off all such plans. The Superstitions remain one of the last great natural wilderness areas on the North American continent. To tame them, to attempt to reduce them to mere playthings (even if it were possible, and one suspects it isn't) would be to give up a part of ourselves, a portion of our heritage that in this day of multiunit freeways and encroaching suburbs we can ill afford to lose.

To others it must seem equally incomprehensible that in our conforming times there are men like Magill, Rhoades, Vloedman, Miller, Looney, Lee, Guidry, Young, Morrow, and Crandall, who would voluntarily surrender the comforts of modern living to take on such an area in order to follow a legend, a will-o'-the-wisp. One might try to explain that while to some the Lost Dutchman Mine may be only a myth, to others it is very much a tantalizing reality. But this is at best only a half-truth. For there is no explaining Coronado's Children. Due to some fluke of nature, perhaps, there are still those to whom the unknown represents a personal challenge.

So the mysteries remain, only a few more have been added to the total.

The falling rocks may have been accidental. The poisoning can be logically explained. Perhaps the copperhead can too, although Magill doesn't rightly know how. But the fact remains that someone riddled their camp with rifle fire, tried to kill Morrow, tried to kill two men by attempting to wreck the helicopter, slid threatening letters under their doors, succeeded in exploding their dynamite cache.

Who? And why?

To both questions Magill and his crew have no answers. They know only that some person or persons wanted to stop their explorations badly enough to resort to extreme measures on a number of occasions.

In a way, they were lucky. Though shot at, nearly dynamited, bruised, battered, subjected to threats, sun, thirst, wind, blizzards, falls, rock slides, a coiled copperhead, and a sabotaged helicopter, scouted by Apaches, ridiculed, branded liars and swindlers, driven deep into debt, and poisoned by cactus spurs and polluted water, none lost his life. Others, questing after the same myth, have been less fortunate.

From the time of the Dutchman to the present day, there have been thirty-six *known* deaths and disappearances in the Superstitions, twenty-seven of which have occurred over the last four decades.

Who was responsible?

It is safe to say that some probably killed themselves, either by failing to take adequate precautions or by actual suicide. Trapped in an out-of-the-way canyon, with a broken leg or rattlesnake bite, or simply without water, some may have chosen to end their lives rather than suffer. It is a curious fact, but a fact nonetheless, that in these mountains everything is magnified, including pain. In at least three cases—those of Martin Zywotho, Steve Hwanawich, and Walter Mowry—there was evidence that the gunshot wounds were self-inflicted.

Some deaths were clearly killings. Benjamin Ferreira confessed to shooting his partner, Stanley Fernández. Robert St. Marie was shot by Ed Piper, and Vern Rowlee by Ralph Thomas, in what the courts ruled self-defense.

Some probably died of natural causes. Fred Stewart collapsed and died on the trail, apparently a cardiac victim.

Some of the deaths resulted from accidents, of which the Superstitions offer more than an abundant number of potential causes. Roman O'Hal and Vance Bacon died of falls witnessed by their companions, and barring evidence indicating otherwise, Nettie Isore Maxey probably died the same way.

Yet, even after these have been eliminated, a large number are still unaccounted for.

In studying the deaths, Magill looked first for a possible pattern. And, at first, there appeared to be several. For example, a majority of the deaths occurred during the same time of year, in the spring. For another, in almost every case the victim was not a local man.

On closer examination, however, neither proved anything. For most outsiders who go into the Superstitions do so in the spring, while local residents, alert to the dangers of these mountains, prefer to give them a wide berth.

The beheadings were something else. In at least five cases—those of Elisha Reavis, Adolph Ruth, James Cravey, Franz Harrer, and Jay Clapp—the victim was found headless.

Ominous as this might appear, one forest ranger to whom Magill talked professed not to see anything mysterious about it. In most of these cases, months passed between the time of the person's disappearance and the discovery of his remains, at which time all bones, including the skull, were scattered over a wide area. There are in the Superstitions a number of animals which might not kill a man but would be capable of dismembering him once dead, including javelina, bear, an occasional fox, and such predators as mountain lion, bobcat, and coyote.

Far more significant than the so-called beheadings, he felt, was one other similarity shared by even more of the victims: they had been shot. As to the caliber of the bullets, the places where the bodies were found, etc., there was no obvious pattern, indicating each case had to be considered individually.

Magill finally abandoned his inquest into the deaths. For one thing it was belated. The evidence no longer existed. And it was for much this same reason, he decided, that Arizona authorities had failed to conduct any lengthier investigations than they had. Unless the body was found shortly after the person died—which was rare—there was little evidence left to indicate cause of death, unless a bullet had happened to hit a bone.

Although the sheer physical size of the Superstitions renders any form of policing less than satisfactory, several suggestions have been advanced over the years as to how to decrease the fatalities.

The most obvious is to outlaw firearms, the instruments used in most of the killings. The problem with this—aside from the immediate objections of the National Rifle Association and others—is that this is an area where a firearm is sometimes necessary as protection from wild animals (although, since the Superstitions are a natural wilderness area, the killing of any animal, including a snake, is forbidden by law).

Another suggested alternative is that the Superstitions be closed to prospecting, as Weaver's Needle was (after the Piper-Jones feud) and certain areas in Peralta Canyon were (where vandals have destroyed ancient Indian pictographs). But with the lure of the Lost Dutchman Mine as potent as it is, little imagination is required to guess that such a prohibition would probably invite sub-rosa prospecting and even more killings.

Perhaps little can be done, except what the sheriffs of Maricopa and Pinal counties now do: ask visitors to the Superstitions to register with either of their offices (in Phoenix and Florence) before going in and after coming out and caution them that they enter these mountains at their own risk.

Unpleasant though it is, the fact remains that there have been a large number of unexplained deaths and disappearances in the Superstitions and that in recent years these have been increasing in number.

At least one death is no longer mysterious: that of Adolph Ruth. Shortly after news of the discovery of the Lost Dutchman Mine became public, Magill received a telephone call from a woman who identified herself as Mrs. George Lusk.

The name sounded familiar.

"Are you related to the prospector named Lusk who took Adolph Ruth into the Superstitions?" he asked.

She was his widow. Her husband and his partner were now dead, after years of searching for the Lost Dutchman Mine. That was why she had called. It might sound oddly sentimental, but would he mind bringing back some rocks from the mine to place on her husband's grave?

He would be glad to.

"You know," she said, "my husband and his partner were never able to find the mine, even with Mr. Ruth's maps."

For a moment Magill couldn't believe what he had heard. It was only through concentrated effort that he was able to keep his tone at conversational level. "Your husband had Ruth's maps?"

"Oh, yes, Mr. Ruth gave them to him, just before he disappeared. I have them now. My husband said never to mention them to anyone, but now that he has passed on, and you've found the mine, I don't suppose there's any need to keep them secret."

"Maybe, when I bring you the rocks, you'd let me see them?"

She paused a moment, then answered, "I don't see why not. Now that you've found it, they're not important anymore, are they?"

Magill wanted to question her further, but could see no way to do so without arousing suspicion.

Next trip to the mine, Magill brought back some rocks. At the first opportunity he called her. She sounded upset, almost immediately referring him to her son.

Magill told him he had the rocks his mother had requested.

"We don't want them," he answered curtly. "My mother had no business discussing this with you. It all happened a long time ago, and I don't want you bringing it up again. And don't call back." He hung up.

Adolph Ruth was a frank and open man—but he was not

stupid. If the two prospectors possessed his maps, they had not received them as a gift.

The next time he was in Arizona Magill called on Mrs. Barkley. During the course of the conversation he asked, very casually, if she remembered the two prospectors who took Adolph Ruth into the Superstitions.

"I told you once I didn't want to talk about that," she said sharply.

"I just thought you might be interested in knowing they are now both dead."

Mrs. Barkley said nothing. But there was only one way to interpret her sigh. It was one of relief.

There are still other mysteries.

Who constructed the lookout posts around the tunnel and why?

What of the dotted hexagon, the symbol for treasure, and the snake traveling downward, pointing toward the tunnel?

There is something important in this particular area. What?

Where is the Dutchman's cache? Jacob Waltz never revealed its location, except to say it was in the vicinity of his base camp. Unless someone has found it and has chosen to say nothing, it is still there—at least $20,000 in gold ore, probably in tin cans in a sack inside a wooden box. There is one grisly clue. Buried nearby—if time has not eradicated them—are the remains of a man who was spitted over a fire. Find the body of Jacob Wiser and you will be close.

Still another mystery. It may sound ridiculous, but people want to know: Is there such a thing as the "Dutchman's curse"?

When asked this question, Magill, who likes to deal in proven facts, has to admit he would rather not comment. The author is less noncommittal, knowing that such things can't happen in our day and age. But there have been "incidents." To quote only two on the tail end of many: on receiving the first chapters of this book, the typist slipped a disk lifting her typewriter; after picking up a rental typewriter for the second typist and while starting down one of San Francisco's steepest hills, the author felt his gas pedal floorboard and stick, and his brakes (newly relined) suddenly give out; having to choose between hitting the front of one car or the back end of another, he was saved only by the sidewalk, another hill, and a shut-off ignition. It is possible to go on for pages, entirely omitting episodes in the Superstitions. Magill's own list of such happenings is astonishingly long.

Yet this puzzle bothers him far less than one other.

How to explain the vanishing pit?

There remains the biggest mystery of all—the Lost Dutchman Mine.

Was the pit above the tunnel the site of Jacob Waltz's legendary lode?

It may well have been, but the author wouldn't be surprised if the reader didn't choose to believe it. Magill and his partners don't.

It is a safe guess that had the men removed a billion dollars in huge golden nuggets from the mine, there would be many who would still deny that this was the Lost Dutchman. Another Peralta mine perhaps. But not the Dutchman.

Such is the power of the myth.

It is also safe to say that were the Superstitions dismantled rock by rock, with nary a trace of color, there would be some who would say that this proved nothing—except that the Lost Dutchman Mine was elsewhere, *más allá*. And new clues would spring up, placing it in the Rockies, the Guadalupes, the Sierra Nevada.

Such is the legend's durability.

While it is not the purpose of this book to encourage more searchers after the Lost Dutchman Mine, it is probable that among the readers will be a few of Coronado's Children. For their information, the following list of dos and don'ts has been adapted from the advice of the U.S. Forest Service and from the experiences of Glenn Magill and crew. Basic it is, yet ignoring it can prove fatal. And has.

Don't go in alone. Do tell someone the approximate area of your explorations and the probable date of your return. Do carry more water and food than you will foreseeably need, and salt tablets and halizone tablets, the latter for water purification. Do carry a knife (if for no other reason than to cut out cactus spurs), an abundant quantity of matches in a watertight container, toilet paper (also good for starting fires), and a snake-bite kit.

Do wear a hat and a sturdy pair of boots with *rubber* heels and soles.

Do obtain at least one good map, the more detailed the better. A general map of the whole Superstition Wilderness is available from Tonto National Forest, Phoenix, Arizona, 85025. Although this particular map shows a number of "permanent" and "temporary" springs, even some of the former dry up between the months of May and November.

Whenever possible, stick to established trails. Though they may sometimes appear longer, usually they are the shortest way to survival.

Don't camp in a stream bed, ravine, canyon, gulch, or gully if it looks even a little bit like rain.

If lost, stop, sit down, and try to figure out where you are. Use your head, not your legs.

If caught by night, fog, or a storm, stop at once and make camp in a sheltered spot. Gather plenty of dry fuel and build a fire in a safe place.

Don't wander about. Travel only downhill.

If injured, choose a clear spot and make a smoke signal.

Don't yell, run, worry, and, above all, don't quit.

The choice of whether or not to carry a gun is the individual's. In all his trips into the Superstitions, Magill found no occasion to use his. If you do carry one, don't unholster it unless you intend to use it.

Lest the foregoing give the impression that all prospectors in the Superstitions are killers, it should be mentioned that at least several are complete hermits, who flee at the sight of other men, while one is so averse to violence that for "protection" he carries what from a distance looks like a high-powered rifle but up close is in actuality a Daisy BB gun. Still, the best rule in these particular mountains remains, mind your own business. There are enough natural hazards in the Superstitions without irritating the creature known as man.

When encountering another person on the trail treat him with the same courtesy you would expect in return. He may be Glenn Magill or the author.

The clues are all here, together with the three Peralta-Ruth maps, which appear in print for the first time.

It may be that after giving them closer study the reader will come up with something Magill missed.

Or it may be—and in the long run, one suspects this is more important—that he will just have better luck.

Whichever is true, it will have to be soon. For though Jacob Waltz's mine has been lost for over three quarters of a century, it must be discovered during the next fifteen years, or never. For, by provision of the Wilderness Act of 1966, effective at midnight, December 31, 1983, all National Forest Wilderness Areas will be closed to mineral exploitation.

A last word of warning. None of the hazards of these mountains has been exaggerated. And the "incidents" continue.

In February, 1966, a fifteen-year-old boy was accidentally discovered trapped on a ledge beside a 1,500-foot cliff, where he had been stranded for more than sixteen hours in freezing temperatures.

The following May a twenty-year-old youth, visiting an old prospector in the Superstitions, was shot in his sleep. Fortunately the wound was not fatal. Attempting later to reconstruct what happened, he guessed that he had fallen asleep with the revolver in hand and, in the midst of a bad dream, pulled the trigger.

In February, 1967, a man parked his pickup at the south entrance to the Superstitions and went into the mountains javelina hunting. When sometime later the pickup had not been reclaimed, a belated search was organized.

In March a Scottsdale youth, injured while hiking in the Superstitions, was found in such a remote spot that he had to be lifted out by helicopter.

In late April two thirteen-year-old boys were rescued from a ledge 2,000 feet up in a rarely visited area. Fortunately a prospector had heard their call for help.

A week later, as Magill and his crew were making their "last" trip in, they encountered a number of Barkley cowhands riding out; the search for the javelina hunter, having yielded nothing, had been discontinued.

The Superstitions have well earned their title as the Killer Mountains.

The most fitting epilogue to the search for the Lost Dutchman was put into words long before the Dutchman himself lived. In the 16th century, Castañeda, chronicler of Coronado's expedition for the Seven Golden Cities, wrote:

"Granted that they did not find the riches of which they had been told, they found a place in which to search for them."

Index

"Accidental" deaths in Superstitions, *see* Murders, disappearances, and "accidental" deaths in Superstitions
Adams, Jeff, 101
Anderson, Jimmy, 90
Anza, Juan B. de, 55
Apache Gold and Yaqui Silver (Dobie), 28 n.
Apache Indians, 7, 22, 32, 51, 65, 73, 76, 91, 95; massacre of Peralta expedition by, 7, 8, 51–52, 57, 75, 79, 81, 87, 89; Apache Council, 23, 172; Peralta mines in Superstitions hidden by, 52, 127; and Dr. Thorne's gold, 57–59, 103; pit of Lost Dutchman Mine filled in and landmarks destroyed by, 73, 127, 151, 161, 183; ceremonial cave of, 143; U.S. reservations of, 145; custom of sending snakes to enemies as warning, 145, 146; owl hooting by, as warning, 146, 156; sacred ground of, 146, 172; story of Sacred Mountains, 170–71; Magill's peacemaking with, 171–73
Apache Junction, 29, 32, 80, 84, 86, 130 n., 141, 148, 172, 177, 193
Archeological Commission of City of Phoenix, 100
Arizona Gazette, 13, 19, 68, 72
Arizona Pioneers' Historical Society, 174
Arizona Republic, 99, 100, 103, 109, 133, 140
Arizona State Library, 12, 25, 103, 109
Arizpe, in Sonora province, 50, 53, 64; Peralta mines at, 50, 56, 64; Magill's visit to, 53–57

Backens, Peter, 63
Bacon, Vance, 85, 197

Bane, Dr. Allan, 33–34, 37, 39
Bark, Jim, 52, 61, 62, 72, 73, 87, 89, 90, 136, 148
Barkley, Gertrude (Mrs. W. A.), 20–21, 26, 33, 34–36, 68, 92, 97, 134, 201
Barkley, W. A. "Tex," 20, 53, 80, 97–103, 109
Beheading of victims in Superstition murders, 21, 78, 80, 81, 84, 86, 198
Bicknell, P. C., 72
Billy the Kid, loot of, 5
Black Queen claim, 63
Black Top Mesa, 103, 109, 117, 133
Black Top Mountain, 40, 87, 88, 89, 91, 109, 115, 145, 193; "six guns" on, 121, 123, 148
Blaine, Calvin, 80
Bley, Ross A., 81–82
Bluff Springs Mountain, 40, 41, 87, 88, 90, 91, 93, 115, 117, 121, 122, 133, 135, 140, 146, 153, 160, 162, 163, 165, 169, 171, 184, 186, 191, 193
Bohen, Hilmer Charles, 84, 119
Boulder Canyon, 39
Brinkerhoff, Sidney, 174, 175–76
Broadcast by KCUB, Tucson, on discovery of Lost Dutchman Mine, 175–76
Brown, Daniel, 77, 135
Bureau of Land Management, 153, 164
Bureau of Mines, 164
Buried treasure, tales of, 5
Burns, Dr. John, 81, 119

Caches of the Dutchman, 35, 66, 67, 68, 70, 89, 159, 184, 201
Cactus of the Superstitions, 86–87, 192, 193
Cañon Fresco, 7, 8, 88, 91; in search of, 18–40

Index 207

Carranza, Venustiano, 95, 96
Carson, Kit, 50, 57
Carvings found at Lost Dutchman Mine, 167-68, 175
Casa Grande, 49, 189
Cassadore, Philip, 170
Castañeda, 45, 205
Caverna Con Casa, clue on Peralta map, 109, 112, 133, 140
Cayce, Edgar, 120
Cement of Indians of Southwest, 168-169
Centipedes of the Superstitions, 131
Charcoal beds of Mexicans in Superstitions, 88
Charroux, Robert, 28 n.
Chewing, John, 78
Cibola, Seven Golden Cities of, 31, 42-46, 48, 49, 205
Circle-Quarter-U Ranch, 20, 96, 99
Citizenship of Waltz, 15, 18, 60, 63
Claims: staking out, to rediscovered Lost Dutchman Mine, 152, 162, 163; steps in filing of, 162-63; filing of, for rediscovered Lost Dutchman Mine, 164, 170
Clapp, Jay, 85, 86, 119, 198
Clum, Shirley, 171
Cochise, 64
Coffman, F. L., 28 n.
Conservationists, and the Superstitions, 195-96
Copperhead incident in Apache Junction motel, 144, 146, 156, 196
Coronado, Francisco Vasquez, 44; expedition of, 44-46, 205
Coronado's Children, 6, 25, 46, 196; do's and don'ts for, 203-4
Cortés, Hernando, 44
Crandall, Robert, 27-31, 86, 118, 121, 127, 131, 148, 156, 196
Cravey, James A., 81, 119, 175, 198

Daltons, hidden caches of, 5
Dearing, Joseph, 77-78, 92, 110, 135, 166, 186
Department of Interior, 164
De Soto, Hernando, 44
Disappearances in Superstitions, see Murders, disappearances, and "accidental" deaths in Superstitions
Dobie, J. Frank, 6, 28 n., 46, 111, 129
Dutch Jacob's Mine, see Lost Dutchman Mine

Dutchman of Lost Mine, see Waltz, Jacob
Dutchman Mine, see Lost Dutchman Mine
"Dutchman's curse," 201

Elderly couple on walking tour in Superstitions, 194
El Sombrero, 97, 109
Ely, Sims, 26-27, 61-62, 67, 69, 72, 73, 87, 88, 89, 90, 92, 106, 113, 136, 148
Esteban, and cities of Cibola, 43

FBI, 84, 177
Fernández, Stanley, 83, 119, 197
Ferreira, Benjamin, Jr., 83, 197
Firearms, outlawing of, in Superstitions, 199
First Water, 39, 86, 90, 99, 129, 189, 192, 193
Florence, Arizona, 33, 164, 189, 190, 199
Forest, John Q., 53
Franciscans, 50
Fremont, John, 50
Fremont Pass, 39
Frink, Guy "Hematite," 81, 119

Galvert, Davis, 85
Garcés, Francisco, 50
Gardner, Erle Stanley, 35
Gatewood, Ray, 85
Gentry, Curt: as owner of one share of Lost Dutchman Exploration Company, 189 n.; as member of Magill's April, 1967, expedition, 191-94; and "Dutchman's curse," 201-2
Geological Survey office, 164
Gerhardt, Bernard, 85
Geronimo, 22, 23, 24, 55, 56, 57, 64; treasure cave of, 21, 22-25, 26, 143
Geronimo, Robert, 23
Geronimo's Head, 22, 39, 91
"Gold fever," 11
Gold-flecked rose quartz, 37, 92, 162
Gold hidden under hearth of Waltz's adobe, 20, 61, 70
Goldfield, mining camp of, 37, 51, 81, 129
Goldman and Company Store in Phoenix, 61
Goldwater, Barry, 159, 160
Gonzales, Pedro, 95, 96, 106
Goochie, John, 23-25, 143
Grand Canyon, discovery of, 46

208   Index

Great Register for Maricopa County, Arizona, listing for Waltz in, 15, 68
Gross Lode in Walker Mining District, 63
Guadalupe Hidalgo, Treaty of, 50
Guidry, Herman "Shorty," 185–88, 189, 191–94, 196

Hammond, George P., 44
Harold, William, (alias) and Lost Dutchman Exploration Company, 157, 158, 165, 166, 176–78, 182
Harrer, Franz, 84, 119, 198
Harris, John, 98
Harshberger, Charles G., 81–82
Harvey, William Richard, Jr., 84, 119
Hayden, Carl, 79
Helicopter service to Superstitions, 31–32, 38–40, 141–42, 146–47, 152, 175, 181; attempted sabotage of helicopter, 180, 196
Hexagon with dot in center, symbol of, at tunnel below Lost Mine, 167, 201
Hieroglyphic Canyon, 138
Hrdlicka, Dr. Ales, 101, 102
Huerta, Victoriano, 94, 95, 96
Hwanawich, Steve, 84, 197

Immigration and Naturalization Service of U.S., 18, 59
Indian lore, and Superstition Mountains, 21–22, 32
Indian pictographs, 138, 199
Indians: and the Jesuits, 47; *see also* Apache Indians; Maricopa Indians; Pima Indians
International Investigator's Society for Outstanding Service in the Public Interest, 124

James gang, hidden caches of, 5, 120
Jesuits, 46–50, 138; hidden treasure of priests in Superstitions, 27–28, 31, 48, 118, 143; three deaths attributed to treasure, 28–30
Jones, Celeste Marie, 29, 49, 85, 118
José, Juan, 51

KCUB Station, Tucson, 174, 175; broadcast by Brinkerhoff on rediscovery of Lost Dutchman Mine, 175–76
Kelley, Joseph H., 81, 119
Killer Mountains, *see* Superstition Mountains

King, Henry, 13
King's Ranch Resort, 33, 38
Kino, Eusebio Francisco, 47–50, 189
Kirkland, Frank, 72
KTVK Station, Phoenix, 170, 171

La Barge Canyon, 39, 81, 88, 91, 117
Lee, Carl, as member of Magill expedition, 123, 126, 130, 131, 132, 133, 165, 182, 196
Legend of Lost Dutchman Mine, durability of, 202
Leyva-Humaña expedition, 46
Lively, W. Irven, 21, 52, 73
Looney, Baker, as member of Magill expedition, 121, 122, 134–35, 142, 143, 149, 153, 158, 173, 182, 196
Lost Adams Diggings in New Mexico, 5
Lost Dutchman Exploration Company, 165–78; incorporation of, 165; Harold made president of, 165, 166; stock shares of, 165; financial difficulties of, 166, 176, 177; bounced checks of Harold, 176–78, 182; sale of stock of, by swindlers, 177; Magill made president of, 178; disintegration of "partnership," 182; Magill resigns as president, 189; Cease and Desist Order against sale of stock of, 189 *n.*
Lost Dutchman Mine: Magill's youthful dreams of finding, 6; and the Denver attorney, 7, 8–9, 10–11, 40; main outlines of story of, 7–8; and the Jesuit story, 49; search for, by expeditions and prospectors, 71–73, 81, 82, 84, 86; pit filled in and landmarks destroyed by Apaches, 73, 127, 151, 161, 183; first three trips of exploration made by Magill into area of, 86–93; Magill's belief in existence of, 92, 105; Adolph Ruth's last message on, 102–4, 139, 148; clues to, in Peralta maps, 108–11, 112, 115, 118, 135, 184; location of, determined by Magill from Peralta maps, 118; Magill expedition to, with party of six, 119–150; finding of, by Magill expedition, 148–50; mysteries connected with explorations of, 196–97, 201; continuing mystery of, 202; do's and don'ts for searchers after, 203–4

Index   209

Lost Dutchman Mine, The (Ely), 26, 62, 87
Lost Dutchman Mine, Magill's expeditions to, see Magill, Glenn; Magill Lost Dutchman Mine expedition
Lost Dutchman Mine, rediscovered: U.P.I. story on locating of (1966), 1-3, 155; publicity rights to story, 128, 158; finding of pit of mine by Magill expedition, 148-50; financing of, 152, 153, 155, 156-57; staking out of claims to, 152, 162, 163; and news media, 155-56, 158, 159-60; prior claims to, 158, 163; post-discovery expedition trip to, 158, 160-161; dissension among men of expedition, 160, 164-65, 182, 184; clearing of pit and finding of gold, 161-62; six claims filed on, 164, 170; operations at mine, 166-70, 171, 177, 179-83; ominous incidents and discoveries at, 166-71, 173, 179-81; KCUB, Tucson, broadcast on, 175-176; vein of gold found to be played out, 183-84; doubt of men of expedition that the discovery was the Lost Dutchman Mine, 184; further search for "real" mine, 184-89, 189-191, 191-94; and the "vanishing pit," 187-88, 191, 192, 202; Magill finds pit dynamited to rubble, 193
Lost Gunsight in Nevada, 5
Luke, Frank, 72
Lusk, George, 98, 199-200
Lusk, Mrs. George, 199-200

Madero, Francisco I., 94
Magill, Glenn: quoted in U.P.I. story on location of Lost Dutchman Mine (1966), 2-3; early history of, 5-6; research of, on existence of Dutchman of Lost Mine, 5-17; and the Denver attorney, 7, 8-9, 10-11, 40; letters of inquiry written by, 18; research pattern of, 25-26; obsession of, with Lost Dutchman Mine, 41-42; first three trips into Superstitions by, 86-93; and Peralta maps, 104-18; expedition of, to locate Lost Dutchman Mine, 119-150; and stipulations of contract of Magill expedition to Lost Dutchman Mine, 127-28; shares of, in Lost Dutchman Exploration Company, 165, 189 n.; on new expedition to find pit of Lost Mine, 186-89; and the vanishing pit, 187-88, 191, 192, 202; February, 1967, expedition of, 189-91; April, 1967, expedition of, 191-94; check of, into deaths in Superstitions, 197-98; and "Dutchman's curse," 201-2; see also Magill Lost Dutchman Mine expedition
Magill, Glenn, & Associates, 6, 171, 182
Magill Lost Dutchman Mine expedition, 119-50; personnel of, 120-27; contract of terms of search, 127-28; supplies for, 128; mystery of coal oil lantern, 131; and tennis shoe tracks, 132-33, 143, 146; locating Peralta map clues, 133-34, 135-36, 147, 149; finding of tunnel below mine, 135-36, 139, 142, 143; and encounter with Al Morrow, 137-39, 179-80; and helicopter bootlegging to Bluff Springs Mountain, 141-42, 146-47, 152; copperhead incident in Apache Junction motel, 144, 146, 156, 196; solitary Apache watchers of, 145, 146; Apaches' warnings to, 146; finding of pit of mine, 148-50; making of plans for development operations of mine, 151-52; partners incorporate as Lost Dutchman Exploration Company, 165; see also Lost Dutchman Exploration Company; Lost Dutchman Mine, rediscovered
Magill, Melba (Mrs. Glenn), 6, 9, 53, 108
Malm, prospector, 53, 79, 87
Map of Superstitions, 203
Maps of Peraltas, see Peralta maps
Marcos de Niza, 43, 45, 49
Maricopa Indians, 21, 51
Mason, Aaron, 75-76, 148
Massacre Canyon, 52, 59, 79, 86
Massacre of Peralta expedition by Apaches, 7, 8, 51-52, 57, 75, 79, 81, 87, 89
Massey, Charles, 82
Maxey, Nettie Isore, 83, 197
McKee, Robert, 72
Mexican miners in Superstitions, 50, 52
Mexican peons, shooting of, by Waltz, 66, 67, 75, 139, 159
Mexico, coups of 1913 and 1914 in, 94-96

210   Index

Miller, Jacob, 67
Miller, Jim (alias), as member of Magill expedition, 123, 126, 149, 152, 153, 158, 161, 162, 166, 167, 171, 173, 178, 179, 180, 182, 183, 184, 185, 196
Miner's Needle, 109
Mining claim, filing of, 151, 152, 162–163; in natural wilderness areas, 153; for rediscovered Lost Dutchman Mine, 164, 170
Mining Claims—Questions and Answers, of Bureau of Land Management, 153
Molina, Flavio, 55, 56
Montezuma, 22
Morrow, Al, 137–39, 171, 179–80, 196
Mott, Harvey L., 100
Mountains of the Foam, 32
Mowry, Walter J., 85, 119, 197
Murders disappearances, and "'accidental" deaths in Superstitions, 21, 36, 74–93, 119, 127, 129–30, 197–98, 199
Myers, Charlie, 37, 61
Mystic Mountains, The (Lively), 21 n.

National Archives, 18, 25, 59, 60
National Forest Wilderness Areas, 204
National Rifle Association, 199
Needle Canyon, 22, 30, 39, 40, 85, 87, 88, 89, 91, 98, 99, 100, 103, 109, 115, 117, 118, 121, 133, 134, 140, 142, 148, 150, 173, 181, 188, 192
New Age Center in Oklahoma City, 120
News media, and rediscovered Lost Dutchman Mine, 1–3, 155–56, 158, 159–60

O'Hal, Roman C., 80, 197
Oklahoma Association of Private Detectives, 124
Oklahoma City, Oklahoma, 2, 5, 17, 56, 128, 160, 165, 166, 171, 176, 177, 183, 189
Oklahoma Journal, 153, 155
Oñate expedition, 46
1001 Lost, Buried or Sunken Treasures (Coffman, F. L.), 28 n.
Ore: shipments of Dutchman, 18, 60–61; cashing in of, by Dutchman, 37
Owl hooting by Apaches, as warning, 146, 156

Peck, prospector, and Peralta maps, 126
Pellegrin, A. L., 61
Peralta Canyon, 199
Peralta, Cecilia, 63 n.
Peralta, Concepción, 63 n.
Peralta, Don Miguel, 50, 65, 112, 168; mining expeditions of, to Superstitions, 50–51; mines of, in Superstitions, filled in and hidden by Apaches, 52, 127; *see also* Massacre of Peralta expedition by Apaches
Peralta, Don Miguel II, 52, 57; and Jacob Waltz, 64–65
Peralta, Emanuel, 56, 64 n.
Peralta family: and Lost Dutchman Mine, 7, 26, 49–50, 52, 95; Magill's research into history of, 18, 53–57; spellings of name, 54, 116
Peralta, José María, 63 n.
Peralta, Juan, 96
Peralta, Manuel, 52
Peralta maps, 7, 80, 96, 97, 101, 102, 104–7, 126, 204; clues in, 108–11, 112, 115, 118, 133–35, 147, 149, 184; treasure symbols in, 111–12, 114, 116; Magill's solving of secret of, 113–18; of route from Sonora, 116, 189–90; locator map, 116, 185
Peralta, Maria, 56, 57 n., 64 n., 92
Peralta massacre by Apaches, 7, 8, 51–52, 57, 75, 79, 81, 87, 89
Peralta I Camp, 129, 194
Peralta, Pedro de, 53
Peralta y Gonzales, Ramón, 7, 8, 52
Petrasch, Hermann, 20
Petrasch, Reiney, 20, 61, 62, 70, 134, 184
Phoenix, Arizona, 8, 11, 12, 32, 38, 67, 68, 69, 75, 158, 160, 164, 166, 199
Phoenix Chamber of Commerce, 159
Phoenix Daily Herald, 12, 13
Pike, Zebulon, 50
Pima Indians, 21–22, 32, 44 n., 47, 48, 50, 51, 67
Piper, Ed, 28, 29, 30, 84, 85, 118, 197
Policing of Superstitions, 198–99
Prospectors in Superstitions, 37, 199, 204

Quivira, 45

Rattlesnakes of the Superstitions, 30–31, 86, 132
Reavis, Elisha M., 78, 198

Index 211

Reavis, James Addison, 53
Reed, Charles, 86
Rhoades, Charles, as member of Magill expedition, 120–21, 122, 126, 130, 131, 133, 136, 141, 142, 147, 154, 161, 165, 167, 177, 182, 185–88, 196
Rocks rolled down on victims in Superstitions, 79–80, 171
Rose quartz flecked with gold: Dutchman's ore, 37, 162; Magill's find of, 92, 162
Rowlee, Vern, 30, 84, 197
Ruth, Adolph, 3, 93, 95, 96, 113, 114, 118, 119, 157, 176; murder of, in Superstitions, 21, 35–36, 80, 81, 88, 94, 100–101, 133, 140, 158, 175, 198, 199–201; and Peralta maps, 80, 96–99, 101, 102, 104–7, 115–16, 190, 200, 204; last message of, on Lost Dutchman Mine, 102–4, 139, 148
Ruth, Dr. Erwin, 3, 95, 96, 99, 102 n., 104–7, 108, 116, 126, 155, 156

Sacred Mountains of Apaches, 170–71
St. Marie, Robert, 29–30, 84, 197
San Carlos Apache reservation, 145, 172
Satan, the mule, breaking in of, 130–131
Saturday Evening Review of Phoenix, 68, 72, 103
Scarborough, Ed, 13
Schaffer, Albert, 71
Schweiger, Ray, 80
Scorpions of the Superstitions, 31, 86, 132
Scott, George, 174, 175
Seven Golden Cities of Cibola, 31, 42–46, 48, 49, 205
"Sick-Sac" invention of Rhoades, 120
Silver King Mine, 60–61, 75, 77, 78
Silverlock, prospector, 53, 79, 87
Skeleton of unidentified woman found on Superstition Mountain, 79
Smith, Pegleg, lost lode of, 5
Smith, Sophie, 164
Snake clue: on Peralta maps, 112, 115, 118; at tunnel below Lost Mine, 167, 201
Spanish mule shoe found by Magill in Superstitions, 91, 92, 113
Star, Jake, 13
Stewart, Fred B., 82, 197
Stone face looking up to Dutchman's mine, 71, 73, 142, 148, 173

Storm, Barry, 27, 80, 87, 88, 89, 92, 111, 113, 119, 159
Superstition Mountains, 5, 8, 32–33, 39; murders, disappearances, and "accidental" deaths in, 21, 36, 74–93, 119, 127, 129–30, 197–98, 199; and Indian lore, 21–22, 32; unwritten rules of, 31; origin of name, 32; area favored by wanted men, 38; Jacob Waltz as victim of, 71; two major entrances to, 129; and the conservationists, 195–96; ominous incidents on Magill's expeditions into, 196–97; policing of, 198–99; outlawing firearms in, 199; closing of, to prospecting, 199; availability of general map of, 203; hazards of, and continuing of "incidents" in, 204–5; and well-earned title of Killer Mountains, 205
Surackus, John, 172–73

Tayopa, legendary mine of, 48
Teason, Judge Norman, 29
Tennis shoes: tracks of, and Magill expedition, 132–33, 143, 146, 156, 171, 173; and Apaches' addiction to, 145
Thomas, Julia (Mrs. E. W.), 7, 12, 13, 15, 19–20, 26, 34, 61, 64, 66, 67, 68–71, 72, 75, 134, 158, 184; various names of, 68 n.
Thomas, Ralph, 30, 84, 197
Thorne, Dr. Abraham, 57, 88, 109; Apaches' gift of gold to, 58–59, 103
Three Red Hills, 71, 117, 148
Thunder Gods of Apaches, 6, 22
Thunder God's Gold (Storm), 27, 80, 87, 111
Tonto National Forest, 38, 141, 205
Treasure legends of Superstitions, 27
Treasure symbols, Spanish and Indian, 111–12, 114, 116, 167, 201
Treasures of the World (Charroux), 28 n.
Tunnel below Dutchman's mine, 65, 67, 72, 77, 110, 112, 116, 133, 134, 140, 175, 184; finding of, by Magill expedition, 135–36, 139, 142, 143; dynamiting of, 166–67; film taken of, 167; guardhouses or lookouts of, 169–70, 175, 201
Tweetie Pie, case of, 124–25
Two young soldiers, murder of, in Superstitions, 75–77, 92, 148

212   Index

United Press International (U.P.I.) story of locating of Lost Dutchman Mine (1966), 1–3, 155
United States census, listings for Jacob Waltz in, 14, 15
United States Forest Service, 86, 164, 175, 203
United States Mint, 18, 60

Vaca, Cabeza de, 42–43, 46
Veni, vidi, vici: in last message of Adolph Ruth, 80, 102, 103, 140; voiced by Magill on discovery of pit of Dutchman's mine, 150
Vloedman, Andy, as member of Magill expedition, 122–23, 126, 130, 135, 137, 149, 153, 158, 161, 162, 166, 167, 171, 173, 178, 179, 180–81, 182, 183, 184, 185, 196
Vulture mine, 37

Walker, Dr. John D., 97 *n.*
Walker-Wiser map to Lost Dutchman Mine, 97 *n.*
Waltz, Jacob (the Dutchman), 2, 25, 34–36, 50, 52, 57, 92, 27, 158, 169, 184; Magill's research on, 5–17, 59–62; various spellings of name, 10, 13, 17; last years and death of, 12, 14, 68, 71; U.S. census listings for, 14, 15, 68; citizenship of, 15, 18, 60, 63; ore shipments of, 18, 60–61; information and clues on mine's location left by, 19, 26, 62, 65, 66, 67–68, 70–71, 72, 89, 92, 113, 134, 135, 149–50, 151, 166; gold hidden under hearth of adobe of, 20, 61, 70; caches of, 35, 66, 67, 68, 70, 89, 159, 184, 201; Magill's reconstruction of story of, 62–71; and the Peraltas, 64–65; primary camp of, in Superstitions, 89
Wanted men, Superstitions as area favored by, 38
Water holes in the Superstitions, 109–10, 141
Weaver, Pauline, 50
Weaver's Needle, 22, 28, 29, 39, 49, 50, 59, 71, 81, 84, 85, 86, 87, 88, 91, 97, 103, 113, 116, 117, 118, 132, 150, 186, 191, 199
Weedin, Tom, 97 *n.*
Wells Fargo, 18, 61
West Boulder Canyon, 98, 99, 103
White Mountain Apache Reservation, 57, 145
White, Roderick, 83
White, Ronald, 83
Wickenberg, Henry, 63
Wilderness Act of 1966, 204
Willey, John C., 62
Wilson, Woodrow, 94
Wiser, Jacob, 7, 25, 52, 60, 63 *n.*, 64, 65, 89, 97 *n.*, 201; death of, 67, 70, 75, 159

Yavapai County, Arizona, 63
Young, Bill, 185–88, 190, 191–94, 196

Zuñi villages of New Mexico, 45
Zywotho, Martin, 82, 119, 197